Cosmic Door

When I started living in awareness I started
seeing miracles everywhere. Awareness,
it's really just that simple...

Margaret Jollimore

Cosmic Door
Copyright © 2018 by Margaret Jollimore

All rights reserved. No part of this publication may be reproduced, distributed, or transmitted in any form or by any means, including photocopying, recording, or other electronic or mechanical methods, without the prior written permission of the author, except in the case of brief quotations embodied in critical reviews and certain other non-commercial uses permitted by copyright law.

Tellwell Talent
www.tellwell.ca

ISBN
978-0-2288-0595-3 (Paperback)
978-0-2288-0596-0 (eBook)

Contents

Dedication ix
Definitions xi
List Of Cosmic Companions, Events And Messages xiii
List Of Cosmic Colours xv
Foreward xvii
Introduction xix

Chapter One: The Catalysts 1

    Rumblings And Tremors 1
    April Showers 3
    The Tsunami Struck 5
    Mother's Day 6
    Face The Dark Shadows 7
    Divineone@Pearlygates.sky 10
    Feathers 11
    God's Reply 12
    Cosmic Colours 13

Chapter Two: The Man In The Tree 14

    We Must Look To The Past 14
    Merlin The Oak Knower 16
    The Quote – October 7, 2016 18
    The Denuded Birch – October 8, 2016 21
    Freya— The Norse Goddess Of Birch 23
    Magic In Wildwood 25

Merlin The Magician 28
Cosmic Colours 31

Chapter Three: The Door Starts To Creak Open 32

Healing Begins In Real Time 32
The Virtual Hospital 32
Stones 33
Cosmic Colours 36

Chapter Four: The Villain 37

I Had No Door 38
Bless Me Father For I Have Sinned 42
The Separation 47
The Funeral 49
Cosmic Colours 53

Chapter Five: It Was The Best Of Times: It Was The Worst
Of Times 54

The Gift 54
Infant Loss 56
Death Double Dips 57
Puppy Love 59
The Skinny Guy's Past 60
Best Laid Plans 61
Going To The Chapel 62
I Made My Bed 64
Cosmic Colours 65

Chapter Six: The Water Years 66

Slowly Sinking 66
Off She Flew 72

Death Came To Dance With Us 75
Cosmic Colours 79

Chapter Seven: The Midnight Fairies 80

A Message From Beyond Belief 80
Friday The 13Th 84
Cosmic Colours 85

Chapter Eight: The Trinity 86

And Then There Were Three 86
Ancestors 88
Cosmic Colours 89

Chapter Nine: The Three Gifts 90

Another Mother's Day 2017 90
Trip Out West 90
Cosmic Imps 94
Cosmic Colours 94

Chapter Ten: Song And Dance 96

Touch My Soul 96
Is That You Mom? 98
The Dance Of Life 101
Cosmic Colours 104

Chapter Eleven: I'm Grounded 105

A Setback – September 2017 105
Smoke And Ceremony 106
Cosmic Colours 107

Chapter Twelve: Destiny's Dreams 108

    Endings And Beginnings 108
    The Day 110

Conclusion: The Three Big - A's 113

Appendix A: The Cosmic Companions, Events And Messages ... 117

Appendix B: Cosmic Colours And Meanings 120

Acknowledgments 125
About The Author 127
    Margaret Jollimore 127
Endnotes 129

The world is full of magic things, patiently waiting for our senses to grow sharper.

— W. B. Yeats[1]

Dedication

I yearned to have a conversation with my grandmothers but that was not to be. This book is my conversation with you, my grandchildren —Sienna, Vivienne, Hudson, Alexandre, Ewan, Maeve, Haylie, Wyatt and our angel, Nathaniel Xavier who will listen from above as he waits in the wings. Know that your ancestors travel with you on your journey to the *Cosmic Door* the door to a Higher Power.

Always Believe in Magic, Miracles And Love

For these last for all eternity.

Definitions

AWARENESS – thinking beyond the tangible, seeing with our heart and soul

COSMOS – the universe

COSMIC CONSCIOUSNESS – a higher awareness than that possessed by an ordinary person

COSMIC COMPANIONS – helpers, messages, events and experiences that accompany us and bring blessings, healing, love and magic into our lives

COSMIC DOOR – a portal or transition to a universal or cosmic consciousness that leads to a Higher Power, destiny and light

HIGHER POWER – the *Divine One,* by whatever name you choose

MEDIUM – a person with a higher cosmic consciousness who can open the *Cosmic Door* to connect with spirit

LIST OF COSMIC COMPANIONS, EVENTS AND MESSAGES

CHECK APPENDIX A FOR FURTHER CLARIFICATION

BLUE JAY
BOOK
CAT
COINCIDENCE (POSITIVE)
COINCIDENCE (NEGATIVE)
COINCIDENCE (NEUTRAL)
DEATH
DENUDED BIRCH
DOORS
DREAMS
EARTH ANGEL
FATE/DESTINY
FEATHER
INFANT LOSS
MAGIC
MEDIUM
MUSIC

NUMBER 11:11
NUMBER 1:11
NUMBER 3:33
OWL
PREMONITION
QUOTE
SMOKE
STONES
SYNCHRONICITY
TREES – BIRCH
WATER
WITCH
WIZARD

List Of Cosmic Colours

CHECK APPENDIX B FOR COLOUR MEANINGS

Life is not a series of gig lamps symmetrically arranged; life is a luminous halo, a semitransparent envelope surrounding us from the beginning of consciousness to the end. Is it not the task of the novelist to convey this varying, this unknown and uncircumscribed spirit, whatever aberration or complexity it may display, with as little mixture of the alien and external as possible?

Virginia Woolf[2]

This quote by Virginia Woolf talks about *a semi-transparent envelope surrounding us* that is also known as *our aura*. Our eyes register different colours because energy vibrates at different intensities. The colour black vibrates at a low energy level, whereas orange vibrates at a high intensity. Get a "colour feel" for your experience!

BLACK – DEATH
BLUE – WATER
BROWN – CAT & COMPANION
BROWN – NUMBER 1:11
CHARCOAL – INFANT LOSS

GOLD – BOOK
GOLD – OWL
GRAY – SMOKE
GREEN – BIRCH TREES
GREEN – FEATHER
INDIGO – DOORS – DREAM
INDIGO – DENUDED BIRCH TREE
INDIGO – MEDIUM
ORANGE – MAGIC
ORANGE – WITCH
ORANGE – WIZARD
PINK – BLUE JAY
PINK – SYNCHRONICITY
PURPLE – STONES
PURPLE – QUOTE – DREAM
RED – FATE/DESTINY
SILVER – MUSIC
VIOLET – PREMONITION
WHITE – EARTH ANGELS
WHITE – NUMBER 11:11
WHITE – NUMBER 3:33
YELLOW (BRIGHT) – COINCIDENCE (POSITIVE)
YELLOW (DULL) – COINCIDENCE (NEGATIVE)
YELLOW COINCIDENCE (NEUTRAL)

Foreword

Do you ever find dimes at the oddest times in the most unusual places? Have you ever had the eerie feeling that you are reliving a moment from your past? Do you wake at the exact time night after night or come across the same sequence of numbers day after day? Many insist that these and other strange occurrences, are random events with a plausible explanation. Others, like the author, feel there is more here than meets the eye, that our cosmic companions are at work, subtly working behind the scenes.

Cosmic Door is the author's incredible story of how, since the time she was a young girl living in less than idyllic circumstances, she felt the presence of something (someone) unworldly guide her along her journey; a journey, like many others, full of ups and downs and more than a few remarkable coincidences.

An insightful narrative best describes the author's quest to be "aware" of the forces at play around her. "Cosmic Door" is one "ordinary" womans "extra" ordinary story; a story, that in the telling, might help the reader become aware and in tune with their own cosmic companions, opening a door (or a cynical mind) to personal awakening and the possibility that anything is possible.

Moira-Leigh MacLeod
Author of "The Bread Maker"
"Or So it Seemed" and
"Plenty to Hide"
September 21, 2018

Introduction

Who Am I?

When I was a ten year old, I slammed the door to the universe so hard, it broke shut. Then I spent the next fifty-five years trying to open it to find the answer to: *What am I here for?*

I have no special powers; I am an ordinary woman. I raised my family, worked and socialized. I chose to call myself a global seeker who has found truth in all religions.

I can't see angels, spirits, talk to the dearly departed or perform miracles, as much as I would love to. I respect those who do. Good news— you don't need any special powers either! During my childhood and roller-coaster marriage, I stayed silent amid the chaos and the joys. All this time, the cosmos quietly went about its business and waited for me to wake up.

Why Do I Have Something To Say?

It took a crisis to bring me to my knees. I was definitely in a dark room frantically searching the floor for answers. I had a choice to accept reality or rail against it. I realized that I had spent my entire life trying to control everything and everyone outside myself to make my life work. To loosen my death grip on control was like dropping a sack full of heavy boulders. To surrender to *what is* was a monumental challenge and a relief all at the same time. I discovered the word surrender is a feeling not an action. This was a pivotal moment – had I truly believed I could control my life? Apparently, I did! I learned the opposite of control is to *consciously make a choice to trust in a Higher Power.*

A Study in the Evolution of the Human Mind (1901) by Richard Maurice Burke, a Canadian psychiatrist explores the concept of cosmic consciousness, which he defined "as *a higher form of consciousness than that possessed by the ordinary man."* The *Cosmic Door* opens to an energetic state where we connect with universal consciousness or awareness and a Higher Power. This universal consciousness does not judge. By consciously accepting, surrendering and making a choice to believe in a Higher Power, the *door* to the universe opened flooding me with helpers.

I engaged a therapist for the first time in my life. At the end of the first visit, my task was to bring back a list of ten people who shaped my life. This was a daunting task and I was at a loss as to how to begin. All that came to mind was *death shaped me.* This assignment was the push I needed to go back to the past. In January, 2017 I started writing.

As I revisited my life experiences, I had an aha moment! I noticed there had been people, signs and messages sent to me since I was a child. The universe and its cosmic helpers had been working hard in the background offering support, inspiration and blessings. They tried every way to get my attention, but I was totally *oblivious* to their efforts. Some offered a heads up that change was on the way, some offered protection, some came to inspire, and some bore messages. In awe, I named these helpers the *Cosmic Companions.* How I would have loved back then for someone to validate my feelings and help me decipher the messages I was receiving, simply by naming them.

I want to be that *someone* who introduces you to the signs and symbols the universe sends and validate your intuitive feelings so you know it's not just happenstance. I want you to become aware that you, too, have cosmic helpers whose main job has been to promote spirit and guide you to the *Cosmic Door*.

I happened upon this quote:

> No experience has been too unimportant, and the smallest event unfolds like a fate, and fate itself is like a wonderful, wide fabric in which every thread is guided by an infinitely tender hand and laid alongside another thread and is held and supported by a hundred others.
>
> Ranier Maria Rilke[3]

Rainer Maria Rilke – December 4, 1875 – December 29, 1926 – was a Bohemian-Austrian poet and novelist, widely recognized as one of the most lyrically intense German-language poets writing in both verse and highly lyrical prose. Several critics have described Rilke's work as inherently mystical.

When I came upon this quote I was incredulous. Was Rilke writing this for me? Yes, of course he was. Coming upon this was not a fluke; my Cosmic Companions were at work. His words *"and the smallest event unfolds like a fate"* made me look at each event and experience from the past as a separate thread that when joined together showed meaning and pointed me toward the future. For every step I took, my helpers took ten. It was evident to me they had been and still were guiding me on the path to a door that opened to the Divine — every now and then I caught a sliver of light under the doorframe!

If you have tried the traditional methods to reach enlightenment like I did, without success, I want you to know you also have Cosmic Companions who have been guiding you on your journey to the *Cosmic*

Door. As you follow my story, you will be introduced to these helpers who will give you messages from your past and a sense of direction as you travel into the future. Check out the quick reference at the front of the book *naming these helpers.*

I have assigned the Cosmic Companions coloured threads that identify the tasks they accomplish. A quick reference at the front of the book provides an alphabetical list of the different colours for the Cosmic Companions.

A more detailed explanation of the Cosmic Companions and their colour meanings can be found in Appendices A and B at the back of the book.

Awareness, it's really that simple...

When I started living in awareness, I started seeing miracles everywhere.

FOLLOW ME TO THE COSMIC DOOR...

CHAPTER ONE

THE CATALYSTS

RUMBLINGS AND TREMORS

Poseidon, God of the Sea, used a trident to control the sea. It was believed he could initiate undersea earthquakes and create tsunamis. Debra Doerksen, a Medium (you'll hear more on Debra later), gave me a reading and remarked about seeing Poseidon, holding a trident in his hand. She felt there was some kind of connection with a cat named *Freya*. I actually thought that was quite odd at the time as we had a cat named Freya but it seemed ridiculous to believe there could be any connection? After the reading I looked up the name *Freya* and this is what I found: *Freya* means *The Lady — Warrior Goddess of great wisdom and magic. (*More on Freya to come*)*

According to NOAA and the International Tsunami Information Center, tsunamis are giant waves caused by earthquakes or volcanic eruptions under the sea. Out in the depths of the ocean, tsunami waves do not dramatically increase in height. But as the waves travel inland, they build up to higher and higher heights as the depth of the ocean decreases. The speed of tsunami waves depends on ocean depth rather than the distance from the source of the wave. Tsunami waves may move as fast as the speed of sound over deep waters, only slowing down when reaching shallow waters. While tsunamis are often referred to as tidal waves, this name is discouraged by oceanographers because tides have little to do with these waves.

The first time I heard the word *tsunami* was 2004 when a tsunami in the Indian Ocean devastated parts of Thailand. When I saw a picture on the news of the massive wave advancing towards land, it was identical to the *giant wall of water* I saw in a dream in the early 80's. I had no name for it then!

Beginning in February, 2016 I felt as if a tsunami was slowly building.

My daughter, during her twenty-week pregnancy checkup, was told there was a slight irregularity on the ultra sound. Her OB suggested another ultrasound be done in four weeks as a precaution. When she called to tell me this development, I felt a slight tremor under my feet. The twenty-four week ultrasound showed something more concerning and her OB advised she would like to transfer her to a hospital that specialized in high-risk pregnancies. Her appointment was scheduled for mid-March. I felt the dishes in the cupboards rattling.

My daughter was advised not to travel; so, the family trip to Disney, which had been planned the year before, was off for her. Her husband and the two children flew south while I flew north! We spent the week setting up the baby's room. She assigned me one of my favourite tasks — to wash the baby's clothes and organize them in the new bureau. When I flew back to Wildwood, the baby clothes were still sitting in a bag in the closet. I never seemed to find the time to complete my mission.

Two weeks later, my daughter called to let us know it would be another four days before she would get the results from another test which would give them a more definitive diagnosis. Four days of agonizing worry and longer nights of hoping.

I felt the ocean floor shifting!

Hope

Hope is the thing with feathers
That perches in the soul
And sings the tune without the words
And never stops at all
And sweetest in the gale is heard
And sore must be the storm —
That could abash the little Bird
That kept so many warm —
I've heard it in the chillest land —
And on the strangest Sea —
Yet, never, in Extremity,
It asked a crumb — of Me

—Emily Dickinson[4]

Early Monday morning, the hospital called to say the latest test showed everything was fine. The hospital discharged my fragile daughter back to her local OB. There was no happy dance, as we had not yet recovered from the scare, but we could take a full breath!

The tsunami was heading elsewhere! Still shaken, we went back to our *normal* lives.

APRIL SHOWERS

My husband and I had a good, solid marriage with lots of great times that I liken to being at the top of a roller coaster. Like most couples, we also had times when we hit bottom. Stress always seemed to bring out the worst in both of us. When the tsunami alert was over, we began focusing on our own lives and went through one of those down times.

Reaction

You gave me anger
All I needed was love
You tried to control
I longed for freedom
Your voice was so loud
I could not speak
I was lost in my suffering
You were lost in yours
Like ghosts unseen, unheard—Donna L. Gray, Sooke, BC[5]

The Silent Killer

I stand at the window
And watch you zoom away
A scream of frustration
Breaks the quiet of the day
I don't think I've ever been this mad
Stress and anxiety have taken their toll
Life has to change, or you'll be alone
The blood starts to pound
There's not another sound

My mind was always directing me to do what others wanted and my heart was telling me to give them what they needed — most times at the expense of my own wants and needs. On this sunny April day, my body put a stop to this! I had a hypertensive crisis and was advised by the Emergency Room doctor in the United States that I should go to a doctor in Canada to begin treatment for high blood pressure.

Within a week, we closed up our house and headed north to our daughter and son-in-law's home. During the long drive to Canada, I kept feeling *baby tremors*. My daughter arranged a doctor appointment for me to start medication. Our plan was to stay with them to help out with the children during the last few weeks of the pregnancy.

THE TSUNAMI STRUCK

We walked in the door after a nineteen-hour drive, our daughter wrapped her arms around us and started to cry. The doctor had called earlier in the day to advise the results of the latest tests were devastating—her unborn son had a serious health concern and his life expectancy was uncertain. We all were drowning in grief! I was on my knees each night begging for answers. Nathaniel Xavier died on May 3, 2016.

I feel sure this Proverb was penned with my daughter in mind:

Strength and dignity are her clothing. And she smiles at the future. She opens her mouth in wisdom. And the teaching of kindness is on her tongue and she shall rejoice in time to come.

—Proverb 31:25

COSMIC MESSAGE: PREMONITION

The Cosmic Message for premonition is a *violet* thread. That fearful, inner knowing that something is very wrong. While visiting my daughter in March I couldn't bring myself to take the baby clothes out of the bag and wash and fold each tiny onesie and sleeper—I caught the whiff of death.

COSMIC EVENT: INFANT LOSS

The Cosmic Event for infant death is a *charcoal* thread. A time when all things earthly stop and depression is waiting in the wings. A loss of light; a loss of words.

Now I know death has a shape - a huge wall of dark, frothy water!

There are experiences that change you! The timing of Nathaniel's death and my hypertensive crisis overwhelmed me. I felt as if a giant wave threw me against a rock and I shattered into a million pieces—I felt broken!

Before the tsunami hit, I had the naive belief that if I prayed long and hard, worked and planned, I could manage anything that came my way. I ignored the rumblings of my past — my traumatic childhood that I hoped would float away. Those underwater waves had been building on the ocean floor for a long time. They were a force that combined with the present situation, gathered strength and fueled my personal tsunami.

Evidently, it took a lot before I was humbled enough to accept, trust and surrender. My Cosmic Companions had a lot of work to do!

MOTHER'S DAY

We started our twenty-hour drive to our hometown on Mother's Day. It was time for our daughter and her family to mourn in private and begin to heal. Time for us to recover and regain our emotional and physical strength.

Our home sold in January while we were in Wildwood. We had a brand-new apartment now waiting for us. May 13th, we signed our lease and moved our belongings out of storage. As I unpacked our latest family pictures, I mourned for our grandson, whom we never got to hold. That feeling of having *no control* kept nagging me. I was the one who always made things better for our family. Now I felt useless and I struggled to understand and accept the loss of this innocent baby and the pain and suffering my daughter and family were going through.

Control is not easy to relinquish. Let me say, thinking you have *control* is an illusion. A way of thinking that needed to be burned away. Then I happened across these words during my morning reading — *faith through fire*. These mystical words were exactly what I needed to hear. Now, I could envision the *feeling* of control going up in flames.

> *Faith is seeing light with the eyes of your heart,*
> *when the eyes of your body see only darkness.*
> —Barbara Johnson[6]

I couldn't let death shape me or destroy me, I made a choice to trust in a Higher Power and keep moving toward the light. My daughter's healing journey was just beginning, and my heart ached for her; at the same time her courage inspired me.

FACE THE DARK SHADOWS

At the beginning of the summer of Nathaniel's passing, my sister Donna flew from the West Coast of Canada to the East to pay me a visit. Our relationship through the years was more like mother — daughter. I was thirteen years old when she was born so I enjoyed mothering her. She's known the skinny guy, that's how I'll refer to my husband throughout the book, since she was three years old. She likes to call herself our *practice child*. Donna, at age six, was flower girl at our wedding and proudly carried a basket of yellow and white daisies which were her favourites; ironically, her loving partner now happens to call her "Miss Daisy." His last name just happens to be *Driver*!

During 2016 our relationship was changing in a more balanced woman-to-woman way. Donna's visit was just what I needed, and the timing was perfect. She was a wonderful support and definitely lightened the load. She wrote this poem for me:

Breathe

Breathe in
I will meet you in that place
Of wonder, the pause, nothingness
Breathe out
Can you feel it?
Love resides there
Breathe in
Light and dark
Birth and death
Breathe out
Amidst the chaos is peace
Find me there— Donna L. Gray, Sooke, BC[7]

Donna had suffered multiple infant loss and her compassion and understanding were such a balm for me and my daughter. Amanda couldn't be with us so she and Donna did a lot of face-timing and phone calls. Amanda drew our attention to the fact that the three of us had suffered infant loss and as well as our mother, her grandmother. This awareness of the prominence of infant loss in our family surprised us.

Drinking our morning coffee, Donna asked me when I started collecting items that had owls on them. I checked out her coffee mug and sure enough she had one of our favourite owl mugs. It surprised me when I started to look around at how many decor items I had with owls on them—mugs, salt and pepper shakers, artwork, ornaments and a porcelain vase. I didn't really give it much thought at the time I purchased them.

Later in the evening when we were alone, Donna told me she had seen a baby owl peek out from behind my neck and sit on my right shoulder. I was intrigued and wanted to find out more about owls. Donna said they carry a message to put down the baggage and release the past. Instead of releasing the past, I had slammed the door on my childhood as soon as I escaped into marriage at the age of nineteen. There was plenty of baggage to unload but I had no desire to open that door.

A couple of months later in a dream, I saw the bushy eyebrows and bright yellow eyes of an owl looking straight at me. While visiting Turkey, our guide told us owls are important symbols of wisdom in their culture and as the children begin school they are gifted with owl tokens. Again, the message of beginnings and endings made me think of birth and death. Are we born anew from pain and suffering?

COSMIC COMPANION: OWL

This Cosmic Companion will be a *gold* thread. The colour gold denotes the Midas touch in all realms, a sense of spiritual wealth and wisdom.

According to Elena Harris, SpiritAnimal.info Editor owls are sacred birds and emblematic of a deep connection with wisdom, solitude, and clairvoyance. They offer inspiration and guidance while you linger in the dark.

The traditional meaning of the owl is *the announcer of change*. I believe the owl was calling me to see the truth of my past, face those dark shadows and mine the wisdom found there to go forward. Time to acknowledge endings and new beginnings. A tall order!

Now I felt I needed some answers and e-mail is so much quicker and easier on the knees than prayer.

Ask, and it will be given to you; seek and you will find; knock, and it will be opened to you. For everyone who asks receives, and he who seeks finds, and to him who knocks it will be opened.

—Matthew 7:7-8NKJV

So, I decided to *ask* by sending God an e-mail*:*

DIVINEONE@PEARLYGATES.SKY

Hi, it's me, Margaret:

The time has come when I need some answers. I happened upon Your promise and hoped beyond hope that you meant it. Right now, I am not a happy camper.

As you probably already know, I've been traveling along two separate paths my entire life trying to reach You. The external me was on an outer path that dealt with my important relationships – being a good daughter, sister, wife, mother, grandmother, aunt, cousin and friend. All the while, I was surrounded by anxiety and hyper-vigilance. I sensed suffering, sickness and death at every turn. My childhood companion—*fear* was still hanging around – he and I were roommates! I could easily envision *my father locked in a room* and *fear and I* occupied the room next door. I used a lot of energy maintaining a facade of calm and control. I had an exaggerated intensity of behaviours and was in a constant state of alertness, so I could anticipate and manage everyone and everything that was happening around me. I always had Plan A and Plan B ready to go.

Dear Lord, I am so damn tired. As You know the breaking point came when we had our family trauma and I had a health crisis. I, literally, fell to my knees trying to put the haphazard puzzle pieces together. You whipped my foundation out from under me. Was that fair? I had to seriously admit that I had *no control.* Along with that, I had to acknowledge the silent fears that accumulated within me. A zillion times a day, I voiced inside my head, Dear *Lord send me healing light.* Did you hear me? I let go of my facade and gave up. I wasn't waving a white *flag* as in *I'm done fighting*! This surrender felt like a major turning point and I had a choice to make – I either had faith in You or not! You won! I trust and hope that You have *The Plan—* the only Plan I will ever need.

Now, I am on the inner path to the door to Your Universe, the *Cosmic Door.* This path is strewn with markings, messages and the odd wink and there is no doubt that I found my way. My days and dreams are overflowing with subliminal messages. One phenomenon after another is being delivered at the exact right time by your Cosmic Companions. Woo Hoo—I am finding the help I need. My soul longs for the door to open so I can find the answers to— Why I am here? What is my life all about? Was I *shaped by death?* Can you tell me?

FEATHERS

I started finding feathers shortly after I sent off the e-mail to God. Some feathers were in very unusual places. We were sitting down to dinner at a good friend's house and I felt something prickly under my arm. I felt around and pulled out a good sized, white feather. Everyone had a good laugh at the shocked look on my face.

Another feather find was at my son's home. I was helping out in the kitchen and found a beautiful fluffy, white feather on the kitchen floor. I asked Sienna, my seven-year-old granddaughter, where the feather could have come from; and, without missing a beat, she said from your hair, Grams!

Suddenly, it dawned on me what was happening. I had been picking up a lot of feathers lately and had taped them to my "dream" binder. When I came across Psalm 91:4; I knew, without a doubt, what God would say to me in response to my e-mail:

GOD'S REPLY

Dear Margaret:

I will cover you with feathers, and under my wing, you will find refuge; my faithfulness will be your shield and rampart. Found feathers are gifts from Me and are a sign that you are connected to Me, the Divine One. I have heard your prayers, I have seen your tears; surely, I will heal you.
Love God

> "He will cover you with his feathers,
> and under his wing, you will find refuge;
> his faithfulness will be your shield and rampart."
> Psalm 91:4

Feathers are symbols that have important meanings in society. It can be a spirit being, a sacred object or symbol that serves as an emblem of a group of people. Indigenous people use feathers in sacred ceremonies and it is also a symbol of thanks and appreciation.

COSMIC COMPANION: FEATHERS

Feathers will be *green* threads. Feathers are exciting finds once you are aware of their magic. The main job of this helper is to assure us we are safe and protected. I felt honoured and cared for knowing the feathers were gifts from the Divine. What more did I need to know? I felt I was growing, renewing myself; and, being gently led by the Hand of the Divine to reach new levels of aliveness. Each feather I found made me smile.

COSMIC COLOURS

CHAPTER ONE

VIOLET
COSMIC MESSAGE: PREMONITION - foreboding, can be a doorway to a higher consciousness

CHARCOAL
COSMIC EVENT: INFANT LOSS - low vibration associated with depression, emptiness and grief, loss of light; loss of words

GOLD
COSMIC COMPANION: OWL - harbinger of spiritual wealth; deep connection with wisdom

GREEN
COSMIC COMPANION: FEATHERS - care and protection while healing into a Higher Consciousness

Chapter Two

THE *MAN* IN THE TREE

WE MUST LOOK TO THE PAST

In September 2016 a dream strode to the front of the line as the most profound dream I ever had. I dated and recorded it in my journal under the name "the Druid dream." It was disturbing, unusual and amazingly vivid.

I dreamt I was among a group of people wearing white, hooded robes. We were making our way in single file toward a gigantic oak. A man appeared high up in the oak tree, waiting for us to arrive. As we got closer, there was absolutely no doubt the man was Merlin, the wizard. We were walking with our heads down and were aware that, if we dared look up, our heads would be chopped off. When I thought of the *white* robes in the dream — for me *white* signified healing and goodness. Walking in single file in a *flowing robe* meant I was going with the flow; I had been going with the flow and putting others first my entire life. The *hood* represented respect for a Higher Power and a wisdom greater than mine. *Looking down,* for me, reinforced that I had been a seeker since age ten, who was still trying to find the answer to why I was here. Could the answer lie in my past?

Nora Chadwick,[8] an expert in Medieval Welsh and Irish literature, believed Druids to be great philosophers whose doctrine was based on immortality of the soul and reincarnation. Druid astrology is based on trees. The Celtic word for *oak* is duir (also believed to be the word for door). I've taken pictures of the big oaks flourishing on our property in Wildwood. Their strength and rootedness imbue a sense of stability and protection. Now, I had a new respect for the mighty oak. No more cussing when I fill up twenty or so leaf bags each November.

From Sharlyn HiDalgo's book, *The Healing Power of Trees:*[9]

> The name Druid is based on the root meaning dru, the meaning "immersed", combined with uid "to know", meaning people with this title possessed great knowledge… Celts revered their ancestors and loved ones who passed on, so to them, the Oak represented the keeper of greatest knowledge and wisdom, as well as one's ancestral memory…
>
> Ancestral memory or genetic memory is present before birth and exists in absence of sensory experience. It is incorporated in the genome over long periods of time.[10]

At this point in my life, I had accepted my father was abusive and had no love for me and there was no way that would ever change. When he did cross my mind, I pictured him still trapped in that empty room with the door *broken shut!* I had no desire to revisit my past. Would the trauma I witnessed be passed onto my children and grandchildren?

MERLIN THE OAK KNOWER

The vision of Merlin waiting in the oak tree made me think of a portion of text from T.H. White's *The Once and Future King*. During my twenty plus years of teaching bridge, I shared the following text with each new group of students to let them know how much I valued their choice to learn such a challenging game. I truly believe learning something new is the key to successful aging. Nothing makes me prouder than to see my bridge students (I call them my babies) leaving their nest and spreading their wings traveling all over the world to play this amazing game.

This inspiring text was my first personal connection with Merlin.

Subject: *Merlin on Aging*[11]

> *The best thing for being sad,* replied Merlin, beginning to puff and blow, *is to learn something. That's the only thing that never fails. You may grow old and trembling in your anatomies, you may lie awake at night listening to the disorder of your veins, you may miss your only love, you may see the world about you devastated by evil lunatics or know your honour trampled in the sewers of baser minds. There is only one thing for it then — to learn. Learn why the world wags and what wags it. That is the only thing which the mind can never exhaust, never alienate, never be tortured by, never fear or distrust, and never dream of regretting. Learning is the only thing for you. Look what a lot of things there are to learn.* —T.H. White

The Druid dream was my second connection to Merlin, but it wouldn't be my last. Just wait. . .

COSMIC EXPERIENCE: DREAMS

Dreams take on the colour or aura of the main subject of the dream. Pam Ball in her book, *10,000 Dreams Explained,* [12] writes:

> Herbert Silberer sought to fuse contemporary ideas with mystical thought processes using 'in between states'. This is part of the process of the spiritual 'transmutation of the soul' found in most of the mystical traditions of the world. His book *"Problems of Mysticism and Its Symbolism"*, becomes a work of mysticism in its own right and is no longer a purely scientific work or psychological study.

COSMIC COMPANION: MERLIN: WIZARD

This Cosmic Companion is an *orange* thread. This colour conjures up mystery and magic!

What can I say? Merlin is a legend who went on a journey to find his destiny without using his magical power. When I explore the Druid dream, I think Merlin was trying to tell me to keep my head down on my journey and look to the past! I really had no desire to do that and absolutely no idea why that would change anything in my life for the better.

I had been told by many caring people throughout my life to let the past go. I was convinced they were correct, and I made every effort to stay in the present. I believed that living in the past or anticipating the future would diminish my enjoyment and appreciation of the good life I had. These hints, suggesting I look to the past, were going against my grain and getting on my nerves.

It did get me wondering though — *was the baggage from my past starting to smell behind that broken-shut door! Was this trash causing my anxiety and making me sick?* Then my rational mind would take over and remind me that my father was long dead —-how could going back to the past change my rancid feelings for him.

Druid Peace Prayer

Deep within the still center
Of my Being
May I find peace.
Silently within the quiet
Of thy grove
May I share peace.
Gently (or powerfully)
Within the greater circle
Of humankind
May I radiate peace.
—Lolo Morganwg[13], Welsh Poet

THE QUOTE – October 7, 2016

I awoke from a dream with a quote freshly imprinted in my brain –

SOME PEOPLE ARE HERE FOR THE PAST
SOME PEOPLE ARE HERE FOR THE FUTURE
—MARGIEGRAMS

Weird, I had never dreamed of a quote before. Have you ever dreamed of a quote? I wrote the quote down in my journal and dated it. I couldn't stop thinking about it, so I e-mailed Donna and Amanda and asked them if they thought they were here *for the past or the future.*

Donna's reply[14] was:

> *"Such a simple statement that says so, so much. Which person do you think you are? I believe that I am here to heal the past, past lives, ancestral memory, etc., so that we can move forward without the past clinging to our backs and hearts. Then we can create a future based on a new heart and minds*et."

I was impressed with my sister's insight and hearing the words *ancestral memory* so soon after the Druid dream startled me. Did I really need to unlock the door to the bitter past? Was it *clinging to my back?*

My daughter and I talked on the phone every day, and she was asking questions about our family history in relation to infant loss and the effect this might be having on her generation. She was reading a book by Mark Wolynn entitled *It Didn't Start with You*.[15] She, too, was searching for answers. Could my daughter be here for the future?

I was giving some serious thought to *the quote*. Could we three be here at this time on earth to heal the past from the pain of our ancestors in relation to alcohol and infant loss? This appeared to be a grandiose presumption and I chuckled to myself.

COSMIC MESSAGE: DREAM – THE QUOTE

This Cosmic Companion will be a *purple* thread. Purple is associated with reaching to great heights! Purple also speaks of rituals and ceremonies of importance. I truly believe this was a *quote* of great significance in my life. I felt it went beyond words. Purple is associated as well with the Divine One. *The quote* had a ring of truth and power. All I could think of was the power of rituals and ceremony.

The past creates the present and the present is the foundation for the future! Sounds like a riddle. Could *the quote* mean only those on earth can heal the past for our ancestors?

> *The distinction between the past, present, and future is only a stubbornly persistent illusion.*
>
> —Albert Einstein[16]

Time for me to do a little research. I bought a copy of Mark Wolynn's book. He is a pioneer in the field of inherited family trauma and trained professionally with renowned German psychotherapist Bert Hellinger. Mark writes:

> Hellinger's approach to family therapy demonstrates the psychological and physical effects of inherited family trauma on multiple family generations… pain does not always dissolve on its own or diminish over time. Mark strongly believes to eradicate the pain, the story needs to be told and brought into the light.

My mind went back to the past when I was hospitalized at ten years old for an appendectomy. My Mom brought me in an autograph book and a pen. One of my favourite nurses wrote a short verse that ended with *Every step will show*. Until those *imprints* are smoothed over, family trauma repeats itself. I recalled the coincidences of my father and grandfather both killed in a similar way within four years of each other. Were they waiting for someone to tell their stories? Could that someone be me? The dream of the Druids was still fresh in my mind: *I must keep my head down and look to the past.*

A fascinating piece of information was gleaned from Mark's study of embryology, a branch of biology concerned with development of new organisms:

Embryologists track reproductive cells as they progress through fertilization, become a single celled zygote, then an embryo, all the way to a fully functioning organism.

In layman's terms, when my Grandmother, Sarah *MacIsaac* Baldwin, was five months pregnant with my Mother, the precursor cell of the egg I developed from was already present in my Mother's ovaries. At that point my grandmother, Sarah, who died twenty years before I was born, my mother Florence Eliza and me —three generations were all contained in the same body! Incredible! I wonder if this explains *Déjà Vu?*

THE DENUDED BIRCH – October 8, 2016

The night following my dream of *The Quote*, I had another memorable dream. These dreams shocked me with their clarity and oddness. There was only one other time in my life I had a series of dreams that were *shouting for my attention,* which will be revealed in Chapter Six – *The Water Years.*

In this dream on October 8th, I saw a group of brightly-coloured birch trees—their leafy branches were vivid reds, yellows and browns. In the very center of this stand of birches stood a proud birch with all its branches cut off, rising above the coloured canopy with a fresh, yellow cut where the top had been sharpened off like a brand new pencil. I will refer to this tree as *"the denuded birch."* It appeared to be reaching toward the heavens. What in the heck was going on? I was thinking, as I wrote, I wouldn't be able to make this up even if I tried. Centuries ago, in the Welsh culture, they believed in tree fairies who took care of the wildwood and could open doors to the universe. I felt certain this denuded birch of my dream, was reaching to open a portal to a higher realm. It was quite ironic that my husband and I were just packing our vehicle to start our drive to our home in, you guessed it, *Wildwood,* Florida.

COSMIC MESSAGE: BIRCH TREES

This Cosmic Companion will be a *green* thread. The colour green is related to nature, growth and ability to thrive. The word *birch* from Sanskrit means *to write upon*! The bark was used for writing or painting stories on. The symbolism of the *birch tree* for me was definitely a push to communicate in some manner. The *birch-tree dream* seemed to be making sense. This was the first tangible sign I had that introduced the idea of *writing!*

The birch tree Goddess is Freya! *Freya* was the name of our family rescue cat that my daughter brought home in 1996. I thought of Debra's reading of Poseidon with Freya—still unsure of Freya's role but more to come…

In Sharalyn HilDago's book, *The Healing Power of Trees*[17];

> Childlike innocence can be augmented with ancient memory and the wisdom of our ancestors. Birch offers us a "doorway" into our own strong innate inner knowing.

As you will see in Chapter Four doors and doorways played a big part in my life.

COSMIC MESSAGE: DENUDED BIRCH

This Cosmic Companion will be a *violet* thread. This colour represents a doorway to the light of a Higher Consciousness—movement—openings and closings.

Violet is associated with higher cosmic consciousness, intuition, and connection with the spiritual world — a doorway to spirit and light. Door can also mean movement between two states of being. The significance of the denuded birch cannot be minimized.

It appeared to be reaching for the Cosmic Door —the portal to a Higher Consciousness.

FREYA— THE NORSE GODDESS OF BIRCH[18]

> The cat associated with the Norse Goddess of *Birch* is named Freya. *Freya, as you know,* means *The Lady — Warrior Goddess of great wisdom and magic. She rides in a chariot pulled by two cats and weeps tears of gold, which become amber, called Freya's Tears!* To dream of Goddesses from other cultures connects us with our sisterhood (shared secrets).
>
> The Northern European deities associated with birch are mostly love and fertility. The Norse Goddess *Freya's* words: *Now with the essence of birch you come into the rhythm of life, empowerment of dreams and the ability to envision your possibilities.* Cats will help you see in the past and send help to dispel negativity as you start a new creative venture.

I had no idea where this was going. Empowerment of dreams was so appropriate to what was happening in my life right now. Thinking our Freya could steer me through the dark unknown tickled my fancy.

Flashback to 1996 when my then-teenage daughter brought home a kitten, found at her school, "Holy Heart of Mary High". They announced over the P.A. system that a kitten found earlier in the day would be taken to the animal shelter if no one claimed her. One phone call to us and, although we did not want a pet, this tiny black and white cat moved in with us. She was starving and had toothpick legs. When she rounded her back in fear she looked like a large spider! I had never heard the name *Freya* before but figured it was a teenage thing. The first day I was left alone with Freya, she was confined in my daughter's bedroom, so I could keep track of her. When I went upstairs to check on her, I couldn't find her anywhere. I started to panic and then, as I was about to give up, I saw a slight mound as big as a tennis ball under the duvet. Sure enough, she was all warm, cozy and purring softly. That day Freya and I bonded. Over the years we spent a great deal of time together while my daughter was busy with high school activities and then off to University.

In 2007, Freya, against her cat will, went back to live with my newly-married daughter and her husband. In September 2010 when my daughter was pregnant with her first child, Freya, who was fourteen years old, started attacking and biting her. With a new baby coming, as hard as she tried to find a new home, Freya had to be put down. It was a very teary day for both my daughter and me. All I could picture was Freya crying amber tears.

Now back to the fall of 2010. When we arrived in Wildwood, I developed a hoarse, sore throat, croupy cough; all I could do was curl up on the sofa with a warm blanket and sip water. Talking was out of the question as all I could do was croak out the odd word. One morning as I pulled the blinds, a shiny black cat with white paws and white under her chin and down her belly, was sitting in the middle of our three palm trees staring at our window. She and I made eye contact as she sat still and gazed at me with those amber eyes for the longest time. I kept looking at her, mesmerized, wondering where this cat had come from. It was very rare to see an outdoor cat in Wildwood due to the alligator population and huge birds of prey, and I had never seen a cat, let alone one identical to Freya, in our five previous winters in Wildwood. This sighting brought a smile to my face as I was surprised to see this creature that reminded me so much of Freya. I went off to get my green tea and honey and, when I came back, she was gone. I so wish I had had foresight to take a picture on my iPad.

According to Ina Woolcott, shamanicjourney.com, cats, in general, are extremely independent and combine a high degree of sensuality with a deeply psychic and spiritual nature. Cat medicine includes healing, magic and seeing the unseen. The energy field of a cat rotates in a counter-clockwise direction, which is opposite to the human energy field. Thus, cats have the ability to absorb and neutralize energy that affects humans in a negative way. This is part of the cat's healing medicine. Before the end of the day, my throat started feeling much better and it was the shortest cold/flu I have ever experienced. I never thought to give credit to my early morning visitor.

COSMIC COMPANION: FREYA

The colour of this Cosmic Companion will be a *brown* thread. The colour brown is an earth colour. A peaceful colour that denotes being grounded and natural healing.

Freya's contribution to my life was her sweet friendship. She gifted me with her natural healing power. When she curled up on my lap or on my shoulder, I felt peace and contentment. When a cat appears in your life, the blending of magic and mystery is close by. When I saw Freya gazing at me from the palm trees, I wasn't ready to accept the possibility that healing and magic were taking place. Now I realize our connection went much deeper than I ever imagined.

MAGIC IN WILDWOOD

Back to November 2016 in Wildwood— I found a piece of artwork that would work with our new sofa and chairs. The first time I saw it, I fell in love with it! It was approximately 4 feet wide by 2 feet high and I knew it would fit perfectly above our television. The background was silver, and the bottom two-thirds showed sturdy white birches spaced evenly across the canvas. The one-third space at the top of the canvas showed a canopy of leaves at the top of the painting in deep burgundy, rusty red, and rich brown in full fall beauty. My husband wasn't wild about it so *we* decided to do a bit more looking—darn!

At my first appointment with my Florida therapist in early December I had hoped to focus on the crisis that made me seek help. I was terribly disappointed and annoyed when I was told I had to come to the next appointment, which would be in the new year, with a list of ten people who shaped my life. Over the years, I bought journal after journal as friends tried to encourage me to write a book. I would write one or two stories and when I read them, after letting them sit for a few days, I felt like I was whining. I couldn't seem to make the words I wrote match up with the feelings I felt as a child. My therapist's assignment seemed daunting.

Within a few days after my therapist appointment, my husband saw a sale flyer from the furniture store where we bought our sofa. They were advertising end tables at a tremendous discount. Off we went to the store and, while finalizing the sale I caught sight of the artwork I had coveted on our last shopping trip. Whoopie it hadn't sold and it was 40% off too good a deal to pass up, I left that store one happy camper.

Within the week we left Wildwood and headed back to Canada for Christmas.

I had a month before the next therapist appointment to revisit the past. The memories, thoughts and feelings that I had safely stowed behind a locked door now had to be dragged out kicking and screaming. My daughter gave me a beautiful, light pink journal embossed with gold feathers for Christmas. All I needed now was courage!

Back to Wildwood in January, my husband was watching television while I was reading. I glanced up and was admiring the new artwork we'd purchased before Christmas when I suddenly connected it with my dream in October 2016 of the birch trees with the denuded birch reaching for the heavens. I grabbed my iPad and sent a picture off to Amanda. A few minutes later, I got a phone call from her — *"Mom, who is that on the TV looking out from the birches?"*

As I looked closer at the photo I'd taken, I was astounded to see that there was a man standing in a forest of white birches at twilight. The birch trees on the television lined up perfectly with the birch trees in my artwork hanging proudly above it. Then I gasped— the man looked exactly like "Merlin, the Magician"! When I looked again at the picture on my iPad it appeared that he was looking directly at me. Covered in goosebumps, I wrote the following:

The Magician

Merlin was standing among the birches
He appeared to be beckoning me.
From where I perched
On top of the denuded birch,
I could see the entire forest.
I knew I had challenges to face
His message was clear
To fulfill my destiny
I must reclaim my power,
Trust what I'm passionate about,
And act on the faint voices of
Past generations,
Who have been waiting patiently
For someone to tell their stories
And end the cycle of addiction.
By acknowledging my pain,
I acknowledge their pain.
So, we can move together
Toward the light.

—MargieGrams

MERLIN THE MAGICIAN

It is believed that Merlin is the creation of Geoffrey of Monmouth.

The History of The Kings of Britain,[19] *a pseudo-historical account of British history, was written around 1136 by Geoffrey of Monmouth.* Pseudo history frequently presents sensational claims about historical facts which require re-writing of the historical record. Geoffrey of Monmouth claims to have translated a very ancient book. The related term "crypto history" applied to a pseudo history based on superstitions inherent to occultism.

Geoffrey also wrote another book called *"Prophecies of Merlin"*[20] before he wrote the six volumes of the book *"History of the Kings of Britain"*. The Prophecies were then incorporated into the history as its seventh book. These led to a tradition that is manifested in other medieval works of eighteenth-century almanac writers—they made predictions under such names as Merlinus Anglicus and in the presentation of Merlin in later literature.

In "The *Prophecies of Merlin":*

…after Aurelius Ambrosius defeats and kills Vortigern, becoming King, Britain remains in a state of war under him and his brother Uther. They are both assisted by 'Merlin.' At one-point Ambrosius becomes ill and Uther leads the army. Ambrosius is killed by an assassin. When he dies, a comet taking the form of a dragon's head (pendragon) appears in the night sky, which Merlin interprets as a sign… that Uther will be victorious and succeed him (Ambrosius). Merlin becomes King Arthur's adviser, prophet and magician.

In Monmouth's twelfth-century *History of the Kings of Britain,* he combined the Welsh traditions about a bard and prophet named Myrddin with the story that the ninth-century chronicler Nennius tells about Ambrosius (that he had no human father and that he prophesied the defeat of the British by the Saxons). The word *"Saxon"* means *"sons of Isaac"!* My maternal ancestors were MacIsaac's!

Although Merlin is a mythical wizard, it appears he is a composite of historical persons — Ambrosius and Myrddin—probably 6th century Druids living in Scotland and Wales. Bingo —my dream of the Druids! I started thinking of my ancestors. My paternal grandfather's ancestors came from Wales. It brought back recent memories of the "skinny guy" and me golfing in Wales, during The Ryder Cup in 2010 on a golf course called The *Rolls of Monmouth located at The Hendre, Monmouth. Geoffrey of Monmouth and the Rolls of Monmouth!*

My maternal grandmother was Sarah MacIsaac, who was born in 1891 in Giant's Lake, NS and died in 1930 —she gave birth to nine children in ten years. My mother, Florence Eliza, was the youngest child. Mom's great-great grandfather was born in Smarisary, Moidart, Scotland. According to ancestry records the MacIsaac ancestors fled from Eastern Europe and became part of Clan McDonald of Clanranald. Mom's father, John Baldwin was born in Louisbourg, NS and his ancestors originated from Ireland.

The name "Isaac" originates from "sons of Isaac."[21] *Isaac* was the name of the son of Abraham (Genesis 21:3) by his wife Sarah. The traditional explanation of the name is that Abraham and Sarah laughed with joy at the birth of a son to them in their old age, but a more plausible explanation is that the name originally meant 'may God laugh', i.e. 'smile on him'. Like Abraham, this name has always been immensely popular among Jewish people, but was also widely used in medieval Europe among Christians. Hence it is the surname of many gentile families as well as Jews. In England and Wales, it was one of the Old Testament names that were particularly popular among Nonconformists in the seventeenth to nineteenth centuries, which accounts for its frequency as a Welsh surname. (Welsh surnames were generally formed much later than English ones). In Eastern Europe the personal name in its various vernacular forms were popular in

Orthodox (Russian, Ukrainian, and Bulgarian), Catholic (Polish), and Protestant (Czech) Churches.

COSMIC COMPANION: MERLIN/MYTHICAL FIGURE

This Cosmic Companion is an *orange* coloured thread—magic of a wizard and ancient mystery. After giving much thought to what Merlin's appearance might mean to me, I thought of his purpose. With what little I knew, I believed Merlin's goal was to find his destiny without using his power. My goal was the opposite, I needed to use my courage to find my power. One of Merlin's totems is the Owl. According to Donna, it's one of mine as well and is accompanying me as I *linger in the dark places along with Merlin* and *Freya…* This strongly resonated with me in that it led me to think of my ancestors and some knowledge of my ancestral roots in Scotland and Wales. Could my destiny really *be to heal, not just for me personally, but for our ancestors?* Imagine!

The Bitter Truth

I sit and stare
I hardly dare
But the truth I must write
To sleep at night
So many years
I was too scared
Kept my secrets hidden
Now they've come unbidden…

COSMIC COLOURS

CHAPTER TWO

ORANGE
COSMIC COMPANION: MERLIN THE WIZARD - an ability to make magic happen and find his destiny

PURPLE
COSMIC MESSAGE: DREAM: QUOTE - reaching great heights

GREEN
COSMIC MESSAGE: TREES - nature, creativity, writing — cycles of renewal, beginnings and endings

INDIGO
COSMIC MESSAGE: DENUDED BIRCH - a doorway to the light of a higher consciousness, openings and closings - transitions and connects us with the spiritual realm

BROWN
COSMIC COMPANION: FREYA - a peaceful colour that denotes being grounded, a rooted connection, secrets of the sisterhood and natural healing

Chapter Three

THE DOOR STARTS TO CREAK OPEN

HEALING BEGINS IN REAL TIME

A dream which is not interpreted is like a letter which is not read.
The Talmud

> Dr. Carl Jung[22] proposed everything in our dreams is a projection of self. He suggests we think of the people and animals as you. What aspect of yourself are they trying to get across?

In this period of my life, dreams were like ripe plums dropping from the trees.

THE VIRTUAL HOSPITAL

THE DREAM—I was looking for a family I knew who had a sick child, and I was told by my cousin, Joan, they had gone to the hospital. Joan agreed to come with me to show me the way.

As we approached the hospital there was a long line-up. When it was Joan's turn she went in. As I started for the door, I heard it lock. The people waiting in line behind me knelt down to pray and, in single turns, they placed stones on the wall surrounding the hospital. This dream was perplexing. There's that door again. Was I the sick child?

I digress—A simple incident that happened when I was seven years old came to mind that sheds light on secrets and shame. I was walking home from school at lunch time with Joan and a bunch of her friends. I went down a bank to a gurgling brook to pick some bluebells to take home to Mom. Joan shouted for me to hurry up or we would miss lunch. I shouted back *"go ahead without me—we have no food."* I got a spanking from my mother when she found out what I'd said. I had brought shame on the family. My truth turned into a heavy secret that had to be kept behind a locked door.

Back to my dream—When the hospital door unlocked, I was first in line to enter the hospital. The symbolism was crystal clear, I would need support to open the door to our family secrets. The ceremonial part of the dream, where others placed stones on the wall, was giving me clues as to how I could heal. I needed to let go of the secrets I was told to hide. The ritual of prayer encouraged me to stand firm, like a rock, on my mission to find it in my heart to forgive and let go. If I could forgive, healing would surely follow. Stone medicine heals both the body and the emotions. What better symbols than a hospital, prayer and stones. Those stones were a heavy load that was weighing me down—stones of shame.

STONES

Among Indigenous People, stones are revered spirits. They are believed to hold ancient wisdom.

> *Physical medicine wheels made of stone have been constructed by several different Indigenous peoples in North America, especially those of the Plains nations.*[23] They are associated with religious ceremonies. As a metaphor, they may be used in healing work or to illustrate other cultural concepts.

Stones can move us in certain directions by attracting Cosmic Companions, events and experiences to us. The stone ceremony aroused my curiosity. Have you ever stopped, while out walking, to pick up a stone? I have a dear friend I'll call Buffalo Bob. We met Bob and Olive when we lived in their hometown for eight months in 1974 and have since become lifelong friends. Bob loves all of nature and has a special affinity for stones. He actually made a wall around his patio with stones he found and chiseled. He says: *there are ones he calls just look at me stones.* He remarks that the attraction to pick one up doesn't apply to all stones. When he picks up a *look at me stone*, he is inquisitive at first. Then questions whether he should keep it? Share it? If so, with whom? Is it a lucky stone? Is it a healing stone? My friend Gayle gave me a gorgeous aqua coloured stone from Sedona. She called it *a gratitude stone.* I keep it in my bathrobe pocket and each time it's rediscovered hiding among the fluff, I think of something to be grateful for.

Buffalo Bob says, "*most people are awe struck by mountains, bedrock and stone ledges.*" My theory is stones give off vibes of permanency, safety, and protection. They are also symbolic of *weight and heaviness.*

COSMIC MESSAGE: DREAM – DOORS

This Cosmic Message is *an indigo* coloured thread. Indigo opens a door beyond what the eyes can see.

How could a dream be any clearer than seeing an open hospital door? Clarity of thought and fulfillment of healing the body and spirit were now able to happen. Transitioning from shame-filled secrets to forgiveness and compassion opens doors. My cosmic helpers were guiding me, through my dreams, to trust my intuition on my path to the *Cosmic Door,* the journey to the *light* of a Higher Consciousness.

Behold, I have set before you an open door which no one can shut, because *you have little strength* and have kept My word. . .
Revelations 3:8

COSMIC MESSAGE: STONES

This Cosmic Companion is a *purple* thread. Purple is associated with reaching great heights. Purple also holds the wisdom of the ancients.

Offering stones for the body for natural healing and wellness goes back thousands of years. Stone Medicine applies these ancient traditions in ceremonies using healing stones to *heal the spirit body.*

The takeaway message is there are healing ceremonies we can do once we become aware of what needs to be healed. I wanted to leave no stone unturned, the time had come to go back to the past and learn how to forgive my father in my lifetime. Now where did I put that journal?

I opened to the first page and started writing. When I moved out of my head and into my heart, feelings started flowing as fast and free as a tap turned on full blast. My writing journey had officially cracked open that slammed-shut door to the past. I had a story that needed to be told — the ancestors had to wait their turn.

My Cosmic Companions started dancing and tumbling with relief. I finally got their message, I needed to go back to the past. . . dammit!

I SIT – I WRITE

When my heart is overwhelmed,
lead me to the rock that is higher than I.
The rock is a symbol for a Higher Power—Psalm 61:2

Please come with me and meet *The Villain…*

COSMIC COLOURS

CHAPTER THREE

INDIGO
COSMIC MESSAGE: DREAM—DOORS - a door opens beyond what the eyes can see —a portal to a Higher Realm

PURPLE
COSMIC MESSAGE: STONES – beyond words, wisdom of the ancients

Chapter Four

THE VILLAIN

Introducing the Villain…

I HAD NO DOOR

A long, long time ago, twenty-five miles from the nearest city, on a quiet, dirt road stood our shack.

When my father bought the shack, it had a narrow entry porch where Mom kept her wash tub, a kitchen with a solid black wood stove, and a white two-burner electric stove with an oven. The only bedroom accommodated a twin bed which became my room. My Father and his buddies added on a living room, big enough to hold an oil stove and sofa, and a second bedroom for my parents. When my brother Jack was born in 1953, he slept in their room. Between my bedroom and theirs was an empty, jagged space as big as a window, cut in the bare gyproc. Monsters appeared there at night. I had no door!

The two-room addition had no foundation it was propped up on wooden posts. During winter, when it was below freezing, we slept in our parents' bed with our snowsuits on (my Father was rarely there). My brother and I used to hang our heads over the side of the bed and look through the floorboards to see the sleet and snow flying in underneath us. We had no indoor plumbing. We drew buckets of water from the well down a path that led to my Aunt and Uncle's house. On winter mornings our house was so cold, the water would be frozen solid.

Our shack was set behind a bungalow that fronted the road; and we shared a driveway with the Rafters, a cranky elderly couple. Aunt Margaret, my father's eldest sister, Uncle Nelson, and my cousins, Carol and Joan were better off than we were and they had a car. Joan, the youngest, was two years older than me and we were more like sisters than cousins. One morning, as Joan and I played hopscotch on the driveway, Mrs. Rafter showered us with urine from her overnight bucket. There was always some ruckus with the Rafters.

When Joan turned five in September and was ready to start school, she adamantly refused to go unless I accompanied her. It would never be allowed in this day and age, but in 1952 the Principal of our two-room school, Mrs. Kennedy, allowed me to go with Joan. I was three years old. I can clearly remember the teacher, Miss Hanky, who looked to me like a queen sitting on her high throne. By Christmas, Joan had settled in and school was over for me for a few more years.

Three sides of our shack were surrounded by spruce and birch trees, and the front of the house was dirt and rocks. There was a rocky hill to the left of the house; and if we climbed to the top, the ground leveled out and we picked blueberries in the summer.

The train station was a short way up the road, just beyond our hill. We could hear the whistle blowing as a train approached the crossing. In the summer, it was a hopeful sound. Maybe a train trip to visit my mother's family, the MacInnes in Glace Bay and the Baldwins in Whitney Pier. In the long tough winter, the whistle sounded lonely and forlorn. My mother would leave us alone, take the empty baby carriage and walk along the tracks picking up chunks of coal. When a train approached, she would hide in the snow-covered trees until it passed. One time on her way home, she was stopped by our parish priest, who wanted a peek at my new baby brother — he sure got a surprise!

Extreme poverty is a condition characterized by severe deprivation of basic human needs including food, safe drinking water, sanitation facilities, health, shelter, education and information. It depends not only on income but also on access to services. In our shack, food was always scarce —supper could be soda crackers with ketchup and cocoa, green peas on toast, fried bologna sandwiches, sometimes one pork chop among the three of us. When the money was gone, my Aunt Margaret would invite us for a meal. We filled up on chicken noodle soup, biscuits and tapioca pudding at her house.

My father was in the Army. When I was four, he dragged home a shiny, red sentry box as our new outhouse and stuck it in the leafy trees in back of our shack. It, too, had no door! It looked like it was standing watch for spiders, bugs, and squirrels who gravitated there alongside the Sears catalogue which doubled as toilet paper. When people tell stories of being poor, I can't help myself from asking them if their outhouse had a door.

I was six when my father and his friends put in electricity. To this day, the sight of naked bulbs hanging by a wire brings back memories of deprivation. My father was a good time Charlie. He usually came home when he'd spent all his pay at the tavern in the City. If my Mother couldn't get a lift into Windsor Park on payday, there would be no money left for food, oil or coal. On snowy days, my 4'11" mother cut down, dragged and chopped birch trees in front of our shack. Before she left us alone, she would turn on the electric stove, open the oven door and my three-year-old brother and I would sit before it to keep warm. One day, my brother stood on the oven door to look out the window and the stove started tipping. While propping it up, I screamed non-stop until my Mother finally heard us and came running. I was seven years old.

Absence of doors should be included in the definition of poverty!

To this day when anyone I love becomes ill, worry and fear settles on my chest like a lead apron. Here is my earliest memory, I was four years old, my mother had pleurisy pneumonia and I was her nurse:

Little Girls Do Cry

My Mom got very sick
It came on pretty quick
Pneumonia hit her hard
She'd let down her guard.

Cold rags I wrung
Placed on her head
As she thrashed in bed
I struggled with my fear
Wishing someone was there
All I could do was cry.

There are times when the truth just crawls out—

Truth can be Ugly

From birth to ten
They're at it again
He curses and swears
He pushes and shoves
Glasses break, pots fly
I tremble in bed
Too afraid to cry.

Why did she hide his booze?
He'd lie down and snooze
Forever changed I would be
Abuse, I was forced to see.
Next morning, he's away
No words do we say
I slink among the rocks
As I pick up the pots.

It hurts to the core.
The idea takes me deep
Into a wounded place
With too much space
If only I'd had a door!

BLESS ME FATHER FOR I HAVE SINNED

The kitchen was freezing cold as I stood on a metal kitchen chair at 5:00 a.m. to have a sponge bath from the porcelain basin. The wood stove was slow to heat up. I felt those butterflies of excitement about wearing my first communion dress and white patent leather shoes. The Grade 1's were making their First Confession followed by First Holy Communion at 6 a.m. We were to have nothing to eat or drink before we received communion.

The confessional is a series of three dark cubicles, the priest in the middle opens a small window to hear individual confessions. At 5 years old, you have to drum up sins; such as fighting with siblings, impure thoughts and sassing your parents. Impure thoughts were intriguing, and the priest never asked for an explanation. If he had asked, I would not have had an answer. For penance, the priest handed out a number of "Our Fathers" and "Hail Marys" to kneel and say in the pew before lining up to receive Holy Communion.

Locked in a Black Box

Tis a special day
What can I say?
All dressed in white
Looking quite the sight
My confession is over
I'm trapped in the dark
No one knows I'm missing
Odds of finding the handle are stark

Now I understand what happened. Since I was a tiny five-year-old, it was likely I could not reach the door handle to turn it properly, especially in the dark confessional. It appears I was the last person on that side of the confessional box to make the Sacrament of Penance.

By the time they found me, the other children were all lined up in the aisle waiting for their First Communion. I was the last in the lineup to receive Communion. Within minutes of arriving at the Glebe House for the communion breakfast, I vomited and spent the next hour in a strange bedroom alone. Did I bring shame on the family?

Off You Slid

A car came round the bend
Valerie, my best friend
Came to an end.
Sledding down the hill
The driver never meant to kill.
Funeral home was very dim
Only sound – a mournful hymn
Valerie looked quite the sight
Laid out in Joan's Sunday white.

Snow and ice all looked stark
White world sparkled
Despite *the dark*
A teary goodbye
I stared at the sky
Where did she go
I needed to know.

Death was shaped like an iceberg!

Red, Green, Black and Blue Christmas

Christmas Eve Day, me and Mum
Up long before the sun
My Father's home

My Brother won't be alone
Shopping, in town we go
Mom had a vision
Needed help with a mission
Let the torn linoleum be gone.
The pressure was on my Dad
Would it be ready?
Could he stay steady?

Caught the evening train
Floating fluffy flakes of snow
Christmas lights all aglow
Yellow, red and green
Sparkles in dark unseen.
He didn't lay the new floor!
Fighting started when we opened the door.
To my room on high alert
Hoping my Mom doesn't get hurt
If Mommy should die before I wake
I pray the Lord *my* soul to take

We Ran for our Life

Mom knew the time had come
She needed to do what had to be done
He was on another drunk
Doctor told Mom to pack my trunk.
At nine years old
My anxiety took hold
There was always some sight
Where I was ready for flight.
Mom, Jackie, and I ran to the train
The three of us were feeling no pain

Mom's sister in town
Good family all round
Cousins to play with
Hot water to bathe in
Food to eat —
Fish 'n' chip night's a treat
Mother's not crying
Brother's been trying
We sleep safe at night
Gone is the fright.

My Mother took a job at a dry-cleaning establishment to help pay for our room and board and we started our new school. We all started to breathe again…

Snake in The Grass

He drove to town to find her
Promised to stop drinking.
Surely, she still loved him
And would be coming home
BUT
She'd made up her mind
There was no going back.

Now his hands were tied
So, he'd make her pay
Called her a two-timing whore
All her clothes he cut and tore.
Like a snake in the grass
He showed no class.

This was reported
His career was aborted

He moved in with his Mom
Was looking for work.
He'd make up for his lack
Hoping she'd come back.
His family let her know
He was trying to get sober
They were hoping for October.

I Got in a Car with a Stranger

I hadn't seen my Dad
Since I didn't know when
Wondered if I'd ever see him again
He did his best to destroy my Mom
Did he even realize what he'd done, done?

Walking home from school
He pulls up in a car
I ain't nobody's fool
Probably coming from a bar.
"Get in," he says, *"I'll drive you home"*
I'm afraid to be alone!
The conversation wasn't long
Before I knew it he was gone, gone

Did he remember it was my birthday?
Or was it buried deep?
Would the day your first child was born
Be something you may keep?
Maybe a tiny nudge from his heart
Had moved him on that day
We had our brief encounter
Then he was on his way, way…

Changed, Because Of You

You neglected me
I needed your care
You fed me shame
Instead of food
You were lost in your suffering
And couldn't know mine

We were both lost

Three o'clock – end of class
Run to church 'cross frozen grass
For him I pray
This cold November day
Two hours later supper is ready
We're coming slow and steady
The phone gives a jingle
I get a tingle!
The news is bad
Gone is my Dad
Should I be sad, sad

THE SEPARATION

June 1959 was the date my parents separated. That September 1959, I started Grade IV at St. Joseph Catholic Girls' School adjacent to the Church. My brother Jackie was at Alexander MacKay Boys School across the street. It was my first year having a nun for a teacher. Sister Ann Veronica was petite, with kind, doe eyes. I imagined hiding in the folds of her habit and being swished over to the convent, so I could live with her among the nuns and absorb the sense of peace, safety and solitude I sensed in her.

I had no idea what possessed me but after class, as my cousins were walking home, I headed to the Church. It was one of the darkest and coldest November days.

The main floor of the Church had been destroyed in a fire; therefore, the basement was being used until new construction could begin in the spring. The entry was dark and smelled slightly musty (a smell I despise to this day). A double set of stairs went down to the temporary church which was almost as dark as the entry. If not for the flickering candles, lit in remembrance of the departed, it would have been dangerously dark. Oil soap and incense, leftover from the noon Benediction, floated just above my head and I felt comforted. The Church was eerily empty.

I strode briskly and boldly to the altar.

I genuflected, knelt on the wooden kneeler and started to pray. The statue of the crucified Christ was on my left side. He wore a crown of thorns and the blood trickled down his face. The bloody spear marks in his sides spoke of His agony. My only prayer that day was *Lord, please take care of my Father*. I had learned in religion class that if you prayed and made a sacrifice, you had a better chance of having your request answered. To seal the deal, I kept my mittens in the pocket of my hooded jacket for the four blocks to my Aunt's place.

Did I love my father? Did I want to live in a house with him again. The answer to both those questions would be a big, fat "NO"! Now as an adult writing this, I realize that I was only a ten year old child, but I felt all grown up. I had no idea, at that time, what possessed me to go to the church on that particular day.

An hour or so after I got back, Aunt Barb called everyone to supper. She ran the apartment with an iron fist and slowpokes got the dregs. Nine of us headed to the kitchen table while Aunt Barb got the baby into the high chair. We had just started to dig into our mulligan stew when the phone rang. Immediately, I got up and locked myself in the bathroom. I already knew the news would be bad. After my Mom left for the hospital, my Aunt coaxed me out of the bathroom. Without another word, she took my hand and led me to one of the two bedrooms, where we knelt in front of a bureau and prayed the rosary together. A fluorescent statue of the Blessed Virgin solemnly stood watch.

Later, we found out from Aunt Gloria, my Dad's youngest sibling, my father had gone to the City to look for work dressed smartly in his gray flannels and navy-blue blazer. She told us he was no longer drinking and was interviewing for a job, so he could make a fresh start with my Mother. After his job interview, he took the blue and white bus which stopped directly across the street from his parent's house. He walked out from behind the bus and was struck by a car driving in the opposite direction. Then a car coming in his direction hit him and dragged him about 30 yards. He died in the ambulance on the way to the hospital—November 30, 1959.

Sadly, Aunt Gloria who was only ten years older than me, saw the accident from the living room window.

THE FUNERAL

I stood in wonder as the green army vehicles and limos surrounded the entire Gate of Heaven Cemetery. I am not sure why he was given a twenty-one-gun salute and the pomp and circumstance, but apparently whatever happened with his military job between July and November will remain a mystery to me.

What I remember most about the day is riding in the black limo and wondering why the people I saw were carrying on as usual. Didn't they know this day was suspended between two worlds – the past and the future? How could people keep doing ordinary things, like waiting for a bus, riding on a bicycle or carrying bags of groceries to their cars? It felt like "time had stopped"! Deep in my soul, knew I would be changed forever. Was it good? Or was it bad? It just was!

I had so many questions but no answers. Would I be a kid ever again? Where did my father go? Why did my father go? Who will be next? Will I be next? Did God misinterpret my prayers when I prayed for him to take care of my father? Did God think that the only way he could take care of him was to take his soul? Was I bewitched? Was it my fault? Ever since that experience, wording prayers creates a visceral sensation of fear.

For the next three months, I wore a black armband on my white school blouse; and Jackie, who was six, wore a black bow tie to school as a sign of mourning. The black armband reminded me of the coal my mother picked off the railway tracks on those snowy, winter days.

Death is shaped like jagged black coal!

COSMIC EVENT: DEATH

Death will be a *black* thread. Black is the colour of the unknown, grief, fear and mourning.

Death opens a space that can never be filled. When death bows your head, there's a room in your heart where you go to find comfort.

Black is perfect because it is not a colour. When you are in mourning, you feel colourless. A black object absorbs all the colours of the visible spectrum and reflects none of them to the eyes. When time resumes, healing begins as nature's colours claim you, calm you and help restore you. Can death also shape you?

COSMIC MESSAGE: PREMONITION

This Cosmic Message will be a *violet* thread. This colour represents a doorway to the light of a higher consciousness – transitions and connections.

Have you ever said out loud or thought quietly to yourself —*I have a bad feeling!* Or *something just doesn't feel right!* Or *I need to do this now*! My visit to the church was totally one of those moments—*I need to do this now!*

Violet denotes the psychic power of attunement. Feelings of foreboding alert you to premonition. That feeling that comes out of nowhere and would be a perfect descriptor of my experience on November 30, 1959.

A few weeks after…

Angel in White

My appendix must come out
Lots of pain, I don't shout
I feel safe and secure
My room has a door

Nurse laid 'cross my bed
Snowflakes drifting lazily
Turning the lit courtyard
Into a winter wonderland
Stillness and peace
Pure beauty
Ice and cold
Warm connections
Never grow old

In my autograph book, my Nurse did write…

Your future lies before you
like a sheet of driven snow
Be careful how you step in it
For every step will show

—Unknown

COSMIC COMPANION: EARTH ANGELS

This Cosmic Companion will be a *white* thread. *White* is associated with goodness, purity, healing and safety.

I feel in my heart my nurse was an Earth Angel. She came into my life when I needed a sense of safety and guidance. Her message to me was to go forward; but to pause every now and again to look back to check that I was on the right path. She showed me caring and love by sharing her *presence,* the greatest gift of all.

I believe there are human beings who are highly evolved spiritually, who come to earth to carry out God's work. They usually have no conscious idea that that's what their role is. My cosmic companion was there for me in a time of great need.

When you look back on your life, certain people will stand out as being there for you and supporting you in the *exact right way!* They leave a permanent imprint on your soul. Earth Angels Walk Among Us!

COSMIC COLOURS

CHAPTER FOUR

BLACK
COSMIC EVENT: DEATH – shaped like jagged, black coal

VIOLET
COSMIC MESSAGE: PREMONITION — foreboding, an inner knowing

WHITE
COSMIC COMPANION: EARTH ANGEL —healing, safety and care

Chapter Five

IT WAS THE BEST OF TIMES:
IT WAS THE WORST OF TIMES

THE GIFT

When my new step-father was fourteen years old he was diagnosed with tuberculosis and spent 16 years in a Sanatorium. He was discharged, at thirty years old minus one lung. He secured a steady job at the Halifax Dockyard in the radio repair shop. When he married my Mother in 1960, he was thirty-six years old, in good health and drove a bright yellow Studebaker.

The Next Ten Years of My Life

I called him Papa – Chester was his name
Gentleness and kindness was his game
In the Fall of '60, we had a new home
We hoped never again to be alone
At birth, they lost their firstborn son
We hoped they'd have another one
Fall of '62, Donna came that year
That birth went well; she was a dear
Mom started drinking

Weekend case of beer
Then more and more
Bootleggers knocked on our door
Our lives were shaken to the core
Papa did everything he could
Mom did nothing she should
She'd gotten us a home
She couldn't raise us alone
But *Oh, what a price!*
She couldn't be nice.

There was absolutely no doubt that Jackie and I were gifted with a hard-working, reliable step-father who showed us that he could be trusted to support us. Jackie was a rambunctious boy and Papa found it very stressful as he transitioned into an instant father with an eleven and seven-year-old. Sadly Jackie and Papa never formed a father/son bond. As I look back now, I realize my brother, (given name "John"), carried not only the name of his father, but his maternal and paternal grandfathers, as well as his maternal and paternal great-grandfathers. He carried *the curse* of the ancestors.

Being a quiet, studious girl Papa and I hit it off immediately. He told me, when I was an adult, that he had felt an instant connection with me the first time he saw me. Sharing a common interest in music helped us establish a wonderful father/daughter relationship. He introduced me to Mario Lanza and Edith Piaf. We watched old musicals like *Singing in the Rain,* Debbie Reynolds, Donald O'Connor and Gene Kelly; *Indian Love Call,* Jeanette MacDonald and Nelson Eddy; and *Rose Marie,* Ann Blyth and Howard Keel.

Every Christmas Eve we watched *A Christmas Carol* by Charles Dickens. Papa, sitting in his lazy boy wearing one of his beige cardigans, cried every year at the part where Ebenezer Scrooge sees the light and buys a turkey for the Cratchits. We always had a good laugh at his expense. Then he would end up laughing and crying at the same time—all the while his shoulders heaving. He would bring out his special bottle of sherry while we found the tissues. Then we were all allowed to have a sip, in a shot glass, to toast the season.

A seed hidden in the heart of an apple is an orchard invisible.
—Welsh Proverb

INFANT LOSS

I clearly remember coming home from school to find out from our neighbour, Bonita, that my Mom had gone to the hospital and would bring home a new baby. I went to my bedroom and wedged myself between the wall and the bed, gazed at the ceiling and prayed hard that God would let my Mother live. I have no idea why I thought she would die. I made a promise that day, at twelve years old, to become a nun. A few days later my Mom came home with empty arms and said that Laurie, our baby brother, was now an angel in heaven. I overheard her telling Bonita that when the baby was delivered his intestines formed outside his body and she went into shock. While in shock, she had a rather scary vision of my late father. When she finally came back to consciousness, the nurses were pouring buckets of ice over her and told her they thought they'd lost her.

By the time I turned 15, my mother had become a binge alcoholic. When she was sober, she was very, very good. You could find her in the small galley kitchen with a red polka dot scarf on her head so, heaven forbid, she wouldn't get hair in the food. She loved to make big pots of stew, pea soup, spaghetti sauce and meatloaf. She turned out apple pies, lemon squares and tea biscuits for us and the elderly widow-lady across the hall. I love having a pot of soup simmering on the back of the stove.

When Mom was drunk, she was awful! Ready to pick a fight if you looked at her crooked! Thank goodness she took to her bedroom and didn't leave the apartment. Each year her longest binge was from my birthday, October 30 to January 2. Her best time of year was the 40 days during Lent. I felt as if I was living with Dr. Jekyll and Mrs. Hyde.

COSMIC EVENT: INFANT LOSS

This event is a *charcoal* thread. Charcoal is a *dark gray* colour. The first recorded use of the word charcoal, *as a colour,* was in England in 1606. This colour has a low luminance and is associated with depression.

Death smelled like smokey ashes!

COSMIC COMPANION: EARTH ANGEL

This Cosmic Companion is a *white* thread.

My Papa was an Earth Angel sent to love and protect me. He offered the gift of a father's love. When he suffered from headaches, I would rub his forehead. He told me because my hands were light as feathers, they made his headache fly away. He made my heart sing.

DEATH DOUBLE DIPS

The Last Dance

Don Messer and
His Islanders
Came on TV at 7:30 pm
At 63 Grannie loved to dance
to fiddle music,

she would prance
At 3:00 am
She put up no fight
Her heart gave out
Without a shout

The Blue and White Bus

Grandad felt life was insane
He wanted out of the game
Grannie no longer there
Just an empty chair.
Took the bus to town
Drinking the misery down.
Pitch black in the rain
He stepped off the bus
The driver didn't see him
He was gone with no fuss
There are no words to say
Gone the same way!

Death has a shape —a blue and white bus!

COSMIC MESSAGE: COINCIDENCE

This Cosmic Message is a *dull yellow* thread. Dull yellow denotes a negative coincidence and signifies low vibrations.

A coincidence is a remarkable concurrence of events or circumstances without apparent causal connection. Four years after my father was killed stepping off an Acadian Lines bus, my grandfather dies the same way! A bizarre coincidence? A cosmic message?

I came to a startling conclusion that alcohol, either indirectly or directly, played a huge roll in my father's and my grandfather's death. This message will become much clearer as my story unfolds and is linked to ancestral healing.

PUPPY LOVE

The very first time I saw the *skinny guy* was at a party. I was thirteen years old and staying for the weekend at my cousin's house in the City. We went to a birthday party for one of her friends who lived in her neighbourhood. I caught sight of this tall, good-looking guy who was cracking jokes and making everyone laugh. I didn't know why but I felt an instant attraction. After the party, when my cousin and I settled in for the night, I confided in her that I would marry him. She just laughed.

I was a very sensible girl, serious and straight as a dye. I was good friends with two boys at my school. In other words, this sudden feeling for the skinny guy was not precipitated by a longing for a boyfriend and took me by surprise.

> My cousin invited me to town
> To a party we would go
> And I ran smack into him
> He was acting like a clown
> Without a second thought
> I fell for his charm
> Surely a stolen kiss
> Could do no harm

My Stepfather worked in the City and it was a forty minute drive back and forth from home to work. When I was fifteen years old, we moved into Halifax. The house my parents rented was five minutes from my Papa's work and guess who lived directly across the street from me —the skinny guy!

> Two years had gone by
> Before I saw him again
> When we left the country
> And moved to the City
> That guy I met in '62
> That guy I thought was sweet
> Lived right across the street

I joined Air Cadets as Marlene, my cousin, was a recruit. You'll never guess, but that guy I claimed I would marry was also an Air Cadet, and we ended being the last two to walk home together. He liked to tease me and told all his friends *I stalked him*.

He gave me his ring on August 26, 1966. We were officially *going steady*. We have never wavered from that commitment to each other and are forever entwined!

> *When I saw you, I fell in love, and then you smiled because you knew.* —Shakespeare[24]

THE SKINNY GUY'S PAST

This guy I fell in love with lived in a low-income housing project with his parents and two younger brothers, directly across the street from my parents' small bungalow. He had lots of ambition and was quite handsome, charming and smart – he skipped a grade in school. He wanted to go to University and take science, his favourite subject. Unfortunately, in his last year of high school, his father, at 40 years old, was diagnosed with a terminal illness.

His Dad, Earl, worked in construction but had no disability pension. He had to stop working as his illness progressed. His Mom, Bette, who was extremely frugal, did her best to keep the family fed. She did love to sew and put that skill to use. The skinny guy was forced to go door-to-door selling aprons! He still hasn't gotten over the embarrassment he felt as a teenage boy knocking on doors selling aprons for $2 apiece. When the skinny guy finished high school at age 18, he completed a Certificate in Accounting and started work to help support his family. Sadly, late September 1968 my future father-in-law passed away on the day after his 42nd birthday.

COSMIC COMPANION: WITCH

This Cosmic Companion will be an ORANGE thread. The colour *orange* is a hot colour. Enthusiasm, fascination and creativity all encompass the colour orange. An ability to make magic happen.

I believe my mother-in-law (MIL) had *psychic powers.* She had a fascination with the astrology and liked to read tea leaves and chart out horoscopes. Unfortunately, she also had an irrational fear of opening her heart and home to others which blocked her progress and enjoyment of life. I know we all joke about our MIL's being *witches,* but I must say I considered her a good witch and we got along fine for 53 years.

BEST LAID PLANS

We set our wedding date for August 26, 1969 — that date was special as it was the anniversary of when we started going steady and the date we became engaged in 1968. On New Year's Eve 1968 we had permission to sleep over at a married friend's apartment as we were going to a party. When we all staggered back to the apartment, the skinny guy was overjoyed to see a blow-up double bed set up for us on the living room floor! Need I say more.

March 1969 my Doctor confirmed I was pregnant and due mid-October. Our announcement that we were changing our wedding date from August 26th to April 26th elicited a few memorable comments from our parents.

My Mom – *You just couldn't wait, could you? You little fool!*
My Stepfather – *I knew nothing good was going to come from you both staying out so late in the closed-in-porch*!
My future MIL – *You made your bed, now lie in it!*

GOING TO THE CHAPEL

We were married on the evening of Saturday April 26, 1969 in St. Joseph's Church, Halifax. This was the Church I ran to the day my father was killed. It also happened to be the family church for my father's parents and grandparents, which I only found out recently.

We had no honeymoon car, so, my MIL graciously loaned us her car.
There were a few strings attached:

1. We had to wait until she, her mother and sister were ready to leave our wedding reception, so we could drive them all home.
2. We had to have the Comet back on Monday at noon as it was scheduled to have a panel painted.

The skinny guy and I dropped his family off at 1:30 in the morning. My gorgeous new husband, dressed in a white tuxedo with a red rose in his lapel, and I headed out of the City. We drove for half an hour, passing quite a few nice places to stay, all of them boasting in large letters **NO VACANCY**. He casually mentioned he needed to find a payphone.

Beside the payphone there just happened to be a very popular 50's style, drive-up restaurant called *The Chicken Burger* that was still open. We sat in the car and had a chicken burger, fries and coke as our first meal as a married couple. Then we headed back to the City. We found a motel adjacent to the highway that had seen better days. By now it was 3:00 a.m.! The tired desk clerk gave us a room with two single beds evidently, he didn't notice the confetti hanging from our hair. In the morning, I messed up both beds for the sake of propriety! Next day we headed to The Sword and Anchor Inn near a quiet town on the Atlantic coast. On the drive, we stopped and picked up cooked, shelled lobster and stopped near a gravel pit for lunch on the go!

Sunday night, we had a lovely dinner and overnight stay at the Inn before we headed back to our tiny apartment in a renovated potato factory. We were expecting our first dinner guest the next night, my aunt from Tallahassee. Aunt Josie's favourite meal was liver baked with onions and bacon so, with a little guidance from Mom, that was what we were having. Once dinner was ready, Aunt Josie had to be seated at our tiny table in the kitchenette before I could open the oven door. As I tugged on the oven rack, the loaf pan slid onto the floor. Without missing a beat, she quietly murmured *"30 second rule"*. What a gracious guest!

> We had good times and bad
> Happy times and sad
> Little did we know
> How much we had to grow

COSMIC MESSAGE: FATE /DESTINY

This Cosmic Message of fate/karmic destiny is a *red* thread. Red signifies desire, passion, love and high energy.

Is love fated? My MIL told us we were *karmically destined* to be together. This cosmic message started me on a lifelong journey of love, growth and challenges. When a strong connection is felt from the first meeting by both partners, *fate* may be the reason, especially when there is no prior history to explain it. The *people who challenge you the most are your greatest teachers.*

A relationship that lasts forever and is particularly intense is also an indicator of *fate* or *karmic destiny*.

I MADE MY BED...

Two months after our wedding, I delivered a stillborn infant at five months pregnant. We named him Christopher Earl. The loss felt to me like I'd had an amputation – a leg – an arm – a major part of my body was gone. In the late sixties, losing a baby was a very personal loss and only your immediate family acknowledged your grief. Our doctor assured us it was nature's way. Years of tears were shed in private. My heart goes out to all the women who have suffered miscarriage, stillbirth and infant loss.

COSMIC EVENT: INFANT LOSS

This Event is a *charcoal* thread. This colour has low luminance and is associated with depression that follows an infant loss. Emptiness and grief surround your heart evermore.

Death has a taste —bitter, salty tears!

COSMIC COLOURS

CHAPTER FIVE

CHARCOAL
COSMIC EVENT: INFANT LOSS – low luminance associated with depression, emptiness and grief

WHITE
COSMIC COMPANION: EARTH ANGEL – purity, safety, healing by higher souls who live on earth

DULL YELLOW
COSMIC MESSAGE: NEGATIVE COINCIDENCE – a remarkable concurrence of events with no apparent connection

ORANGE
COSMIC COMPANION: WITCH - an ability to make magic happen

RED
COSMIC MESSAGE: FATE – love, passion, desire, high energy

Chapter Six

THE WATER YEARS

SLOWLY SINKING

I had an incredible variety of dreams involving water. I would be swimming frantically against huge waves and wake up exhausted. Sure, I was trying to keep my head above water while working full time, mothering two sons and a daughter, and fulfilling all wifely and social duties.

During the period 1978-1979 my 14-month-old son, still in diapers, was diagnosed with congenital hip dysplasia with the complication of having a deformity of the hip socket which required two surgeries and hospitalization for two months. During the first month in hospital, my baby son was sheeted to a Stryker bed, in traction, so I couldn't hold him. I could push his crib around the halls, talk and sing to him; then leave him at bedtime and cry all the way home. The nurses would keep his crib by their station and during that time he learned to say: *I want a tookie!* When he was released from hospital, he wore a waist-to-toe cast for six months. We made many trips back to the hospital to change the urine smelling cast every six weeks. It was a very difficult time, but we were very lucky that the surgery was successful, and my son was able to resume a normal life.

In 1980 my husband was transferred by his company to Newfoundland. Travel on and off the island was expensive and time consuming. The people were great, kind and lots of fun and we made some special friends. I missed my family and the first summer we were there was depressing weather-wise. We had 23 hours of sunshine in August. I wore a turtleneck all summer! *FDR days* (fog, drizzle, rain) were no joke. In mid-summer we took our two sons and infant daughter to a cottage a few hours' drive from home. The pool had never been opened and we had to turn the heat on in the cottage. After three days of torrential downpours, we headed back to our warm house in St. John's.

The water dreams continued — I dreamed I was driving in a car to the point where there was nowhere left to go. I was surrounded by deep, green water. This dream wasn't too hard to figure out as I was feeling isolated from my friends and family on the mainland and trapped by the harsh weather.

In 1981 we were transferred back to Nova Scotia. My one-year-old daughter was operated on for bi-lateral hernias and; during the pre-surgery exam, it was discovered she had a congenital dislocated hip! Our son's Paediatric Orthopaedic Surgeon, Dr. Joe Hyndman, was once again called to action. Another hospital stay—in traction for a month (no surgery required), but a *long* year and many trips to hospital to have the casts replaced. Thank goodness we had an amazing doctor and an excellent recovery.

The dreams kept happening! The waves in my dreams now were overwhelming and each dream exhausted me further as I struggled to keep from sinking. Not surprisingly, the stress of our children's hip problems took its toll. My husband and I were both struggling under the weight of it all. One Saturday, I locked the door of our small ensuite, curled up in the fetal position on the cold tile floor and did the ugly cry until my face was all red and blotchy and I had no more tears.

My water dreams accelerated. I dreamed I was driving my little, brown Gremlin and on my right, I saw the ocean floor recede and a gigantic wall of frothy water was headed directly for me. At the time I had never seen anything like this wall of water. It was a horrifying sight. (Now I know it had a name!) This dream was significant as it reflected my inner turmoil of feeling overwhelmed and ready to explode. Feelings kept rising to the surface and I kept pushing them down, way down. Then I had an Aha moment which reinforced the subliminal messages of my dreams.

Sitting among a group of neighbours sharing a bottle of Sauvignon Blanc, a realization started to dawn on me. They were all chatting about redecorating their homes, what they wanted and needed in their lives, and I sat there stunned. I had no likes or dislikes! Something was wrong with me! What had happened to me? I felt like an empty shell, someone who went through the motions like a robot. What did I want? What did I need?

I began thinking of my childhood. I knew my original family was dysfunctional but had no idea the damage it had done. I could tell you who played what role. My brother, Jack, was the black sheep; my sister, Donna, stayed under the radar but when she needed to be heard, she didn't back down. She has the emotional scars to prove it. Deanne, Mom's late life baby, was our rebel, and I was the text-book caregiver. I thought I was the only *normal* one. Boy, was I wrong!

This realization stunned me. I turned to books and read *Heal Your Life* by Louise Hay, *Your Erroneous Zones* by Wayne Dyer and *Women Who Love Too Much* by Robin Norwood searching for answers. It started to dawn on me, I had to find my voice. To do that I had to overcome my fear which seemed to rule my life. I had to change *me* and stop trying to change *my world*. I could no longer carry the load I had taken on, I needed help. Why did I think I had to handle everything? In other words *I was a wreck!*

Time for a marriage tune up! We both worked downtown so I decided the best time for a serious talk without interruptions would be our lunch hour. We made a date and I must say the skinny guy was a little uneasy. I think deep down he knew changes had to be made but he seemed quite happy with the smooth lifestyle I helped create for him. I kept thinking my "Becky-Home-ecky" days were over.

Say Anything

I'm tired, I'm done
Life with you is no fun
I lock the bathroom door
Curl up on the floor.
Are you ready, willing and able
To put your cards on the table?
I need things to change
You like how it's been going
No expression are you showing…

You DARE to ask WHY
When I start to cry
You'll give it a TRY
We made a fresh start
Began speaking from the heart

And then I had a dream that spoke volumes. . .

Five masted ships far off in the distance were surrounded by blocks of ice. From the shore to the ice there was open water, so I took a canoe and started paddling. This dream was so vivid, I felt compelled to give expression to my feelings of desperation. I wrote the following:

Margaret Jollimore

The Caregiver (1984)

Five masted ships
A dream foretold
Carrying ambrosia for the soul
If I could only reach their hold,
Treasure awaited dearer than gold.

I set out with a need grown sore,
Rowing with all my might
But those on shore needed me more
Could only row by night.
When dawn arose, filling the skies,
My heart could hear their needy cries,
Hoping there would be other tries
Let masted ships fade from my eyes.
—MargieGrams

The water dreams were so constant and took so many varied forms all relating to one another that I tucked them in the back of my mind. Mulling them over revealed that I needed to take action and do something for myself. I registered for a course called "The Process of Writing" at Mount St. Vincent University. I would drop my three-year-old daughter off at my Mother's and, while the boys were in school, I went to school. I loved everything about it. The freshly mowed grass covered in crispy red, yellow and brown leaves lightened my step. The classroom smelled of sharpened pencils and dusty chalk. A nun, Sister Marie Therese, taught the course. It brought me back to my high school years — wearing the St. Pat's colours – gold and green, going to the basketball games and sock hops. I could picture the skinny guy and I going steady and playing our song, *"When a Man Loves a Woman"* over and over on the jukebox in the Chinese restaurant two doors down from my house.

Short-Lived Joy

A course in writing
Seemed so exciting
Finally, something for me
Could this be
A love of learning
Would fill a yearning

I struggled with the family's needs
And knew my wants came last
The help I needed wasn't there
Would try again another year

I remember going to our bedroom after supper and leaving the skinny guy with the three kids. It didn't take long before I heard crying, screaming, then the little feet running upstairs. This was not going to work. I had made myself indispensable and the children's cries pulled me to them. I had to postpone this dream for later.

COSMIC MESSAGE: DREAMS – WATER

This Cosmic Message will be a *blue* thread. Blue signifies spirituality, intuition, inner peace, along with the darker side—sadness, depression and spiritual development.

Dreams send us messages about our emotions that lie buried in our subconscious. Some dreams reveal information about our past and some point us in the direction of the future.

My water dreams were all about submerged feelings that had turned into ice. The universe could not have been clearer; I needed to find my voice and speak my truth.

What amazes me is that the cosmic companions kept the dreams coming until I woke up and took action on my own behalf. They were loyal, true blue, and had my best interests at heart despite my fear and reluctance to change.

OFF SHE FLEW

January 13, 1985 my 56-year-old Mother was diagnosed with terminal bowel cancer.

By the time she went for treatment, the cancer had spread to other vital organs. Radiation to shrink the tumour was the only option offered. She went for a few treatments and then decided she was done with that. She stayed in her apartment; and when she needed care, hired a nurse to help her through the last months. She had about nine good months where she abstained from alcohol and enjoyed the simple pleasures of life. During that time, family and friends rallied around and there was a lot of laughter. My Mother had a wicked sense of humour and she relied on it heavily during her illness to put family and visitors at ease.

We had a chat one morning when I had taken a day off work to spend with her. With great trepidation, I asked why she binge drank. She replied, "When it all becomes too much, alcohol is my only escape." As I thought of her life, it was no surprise she used alcohol as a coping mechanism as she would have suffered trauma as a child and during her years with my father. Her mother, Sarah, died when Mom was one year old. She was shuffled around between aunts, until my grandfather remarried a lady who Mom referred to as the *wicked stepmother*. Mom stole money for a train ticket from her Father's wallet and left her home in Whitney Pier at fifteen years old. Her sister, Barbara, and brother-in-law Ed, took her in until she found work. After she married my father, her life became a struggle to survive. I was there to witness the strength she showed to do what she could to protect us and provide the necessities of life. I can only begin to imagine the courage it must have taken for a woman to leave her husband in 1959. I still picture the three of us huddled together in the dark of early morn as we waited for the Dayliner. A frightened, penniless woman with two bewildered children in tow showed up at my Aunt Barb's door, and you know how that turned out.

Mom's legacy was her love of blue jays. This bird is known for communication, courage and resourcefulness, all qualities my mother had in spades. Mom swore when she came back in her next life, it would be as a blue jay. We humoured her and bought her everything we could find with blue jays on it. January 13, 1986, exactly one year to the day of her diagnosis, my Mother, age 57, left her emaciated body and flew off squawking like her favourite bird.

A few weeks before Mom died, Donna married Stuart in a private ceremony. They moved to British Columbia. It would be a long while before any family could visit as flying was costly and to drive from Halifax would be a long expensive trip—five 12-hour driving days.

My youngest sister, Deanne, who was fifteen when Mom passed, gave Papa a run for his money. She suffered a double whammy—Donna was gone and we moved out of province as well. My brother, Jackie, was deep into his own life and even though he lived close by, he wasn't close to Deanne and Papa.

Deanne presented Papa with many challenges and then a few years later, gave birth to a beautiful son, Dakota, on her birthday. Deanne turned her life around and made great choices to get a degree and eventually move to the West Coast to be near Donna. We were all very proud of her for making a good life for herself and her son despite her rough start in life.

During this period my husband was upwardly mobile in his career and we moved to Ottawa. Our social life was booming. Our children were involved in education, careers and relationships. Parental responsibilities diminished; however, our ability to write cheques and dispense cash increased substantially. Life seemed to have settled and we were thankful.

COSMIC EVENT: DEATH

Death will be a *black* thread. The colour of the unknown, grief, fear and mourning.

Death opens a space that can never be filled. That room *in your heart* will always belong to the person who passed. That is where you go to find them.

The death of my Mother was what I think of as a *bitter death*. By the end of the last year of life she was no longer the Mother I knew. With the diminishment of her body – her limbs were rail thin, death was a blessing for her and all the family. When I knelt beside her bed as she passed, I remember feeling that this person before me was not my mother. I felt guilty for thinking that. Now I know it was my way of coping with her loss. For years after her passing, I would get a visceral craving and, it took a while to figure out that the craving was simply to hear her voice on the phone. We had talked every *sober* day and I missed her so much.

Death has a shape — a bundle of twigs.

I Felt A Funeral in My Brain

I felt a funeral in my brain,
And mourners, to and fro,
Kept treading, treading till it seemed
That sense was breaking through.

And when they all were seated,
A service like a drum
Kept beating, beating, till I thought
My mind was going numb.

And then I heard them lift a box,
And creak across my soul
With those same boots of lead, again.
Then space began to toll

As all the heavens were a bell,
And being but an ear,
And I and silence some strange race,
Wrecked, solitary, here.

—Emily Elizabeth Dickinson[25]

DEATH CAME TO DANCE WITH US

Papa managed a quiet life after Mom's death. Then at the age of seventy-three, he was given a diagnosis of heart failure. He shared his end of life wishes with us and clearly did not want to be kept alive on a respirator. In August 1996 (ten years after Mom's death) he was taken by ambulance to the hospital and put on one of the heavy-duty respirators — the outlook was grim—he could no longer breathe on his own. By the time Donna arrived from British Columbia his condition had worsened considerably.

A few days after her arrival on a steamy, hot August Sunday, Papa's favourite nurse told us he had made the decision to have the breathing machine removed. Donna, Deanne and I sat with him as he slipped quietly and gently away. He died as he had lived – with a peaceful dignity. It was a perfect passing for our beloved Papa. He made the decision and waited quietly with his three girls to pass on to eternal life.

We all wondered if he would look Mom up!

Death smelled like a beautiful heart-shaped rose.

Donna and I cleaned out Papa's apartment listening to his favourite Frank Sinatra song *Fly Me to the Moon*. Donna put on his brown fedora and cozy green cardigan. I donned his sport jacket and Nova Scotian tartan cap and we danced around the living room amid shocking laughter and healing tears.

COSMIC COMPANION: EARTH ANGEL

This Cosmic Companion will be a *white* thread denoting goodness, healing and spiritual guidance.

Thomas Merton wrote in *Conjectures of a Guilty Bystander*:[26]

> Then it was as if I suddenly saw the secret beauty of their hearts, the depths of their hearts where neither sin nor desire nor self-knowledge can reach, the core of their reality, the person that each one is in God's eye. If only they could see themselves as they really are. If only we could see each other that way all the time. There would be no more war, no more hatred, no more cruelty, no more greed. . . But this cannot be seen, only believed and 'understood' by a peculiar gift.

> I suppose the big problem would be that we would fall to our knees in awe of each other.

Merton legacy trust

And the Thomas Merton Center at Bellamine University

Louis Thomas Merton
1915-1968

I saw the beauty of Papa's heart when we bonded as father/daughter. Then I felt the beauty of his soul when he died.

A wonderfully descriptive line of prose from the last line of *No Great Mischief*[27] by Alistair MacLeod: *We all do better with love.* I believe this love we do better with, must first come from ourselves!

I Remember You

My brother's name was Jack
Stamped with *addiction* on his back
Beer and whiskey called his name
He didn't hesitate to use what came
A Cadillac was his treasured car
Usually parked in front of a bar
One great thing he did
Was father John, a wonderful kid,
John, too, had his trouble
Wasn't brought up in a bubble
He is a dear,
Fought hard under cancer care
Lynch Syndrome* is a curse
Put my mother and brother in a hearse

*Lynch Syndrome is a hereditary disorder caused by a mutation in a mismatch repair gene in which affected individuals have a higher than normal chance of developing colorectal cancer, endometrial cancer, and various other types of aggressive cancers, often at a young age – also called hereditary nonpolyposis colorectal cancer.

COSMIC EVENT: DEATH

Death will be a *black* thread. The colour of the unknown, grief, fear and mourning.

Death opens a space that can never be filled. That room *in your heart* will always belong to the person who passed. I remember you, Jack, with love and affection. Dear Brother, you couldn't overcome your "trauma" as a child of woe.

Death smells like Pale Ale!

COSMIC COLOURS

CHAPTER SIX

COSMIC MESSAGE: DREAM-WATER - *blue* signifies spirituality, intuition, inner peace, plumbing the depths, along with the darker side – sadness, depression and spiritual development

COSMIC EVENT: DEATH - black – mourning

COMIC COMPANION: EARTH ANGEL - white —goodness and purity

Chapter Seven

THE MIDNIGHT FAIRIES

A MESSAGE FROM BEYOND BELIEF

My cosmic companions seemed to be taking a break, as all was calm. Little did I know, but they were resting up for the magic that lay ahead!

A series of completely unrelated happenings culminated in a life-changing *relationship* with my late biological father and, yes, I did use the word *relationship*. I can only imagine how hard my helpers must have been working to deliver his message. Quite a few unsuspecting people played a role.

When you get to the end of these totally unrelated events, you will have some idea of what a team of cosmic companions can accomplish over a period of time.

To help clarify a sequence of synchronistic events, I will number them.

1. **The Locked Door** – Spring 2014

I dreamed of my father on one side of my bedroom door frantically turning the handle to get in and me on the other side terrified he would break the lock. Doors, in this dream, spoke for themselves—keep *the Villain* out. It surprised me that even in my dream, I would not open the door. I woke up with my heart pounding. The shocking truth was, after all these years, he still scared me!

2. **A Book Purchase in Wildwood** – Spring 2014

Two of my granddaughters, five months apart in age, get the same gifts from me when I return from Florida. I found a great book called *The Midnight Fairies* with a fairy necklace on the front. Unfortunately, there was only one in stock. There happened to be a princess book but no necklace. When we got back to Canada for the summer, one child got the princess book, the other, the fairy book. Since they only see each other once a year, I didn't think it would be a problem.

My son didn't think the necklace that came with the book was a good idea for his daughter as she had a tendency to have mild allergic reactions to costume jewelry. Without a thought, I gave the fairy necklace to the grandchild with the princess book.

I forgot about face-timing! Four-year-old meltdowns are not pretty. Oops! MargieGrams was in big trouble! The child with the fairy book wanted *her* fairy necklace back. Now on a mission to find another *The Midnight Fairies* book.

3. **Funeral** – October 2014

At the funeral of my father's eldest sibling, Margaret, who died at the age of 95, Aunt Gloria asked to meet me for coffee to talk about my father. I was intrigued as this was *a first!* A few days later, we met. She wanted to explain that she believed my father suffered from PTSD. She felt this caused his irresponsibility, abuse and neglect. More importantly, she wanted me to know that he loved me. With absolutely no hesitation and a certain amount of arrogance, I told her his actions spoke louder than any words she could ever say and there would be nothing I could ever imagine redeeming him in my eyes. I had felt no love from him or for him and considered him a *father in name only*. I wondered to myself why on earth she was bringing this up since he'd been dead for 54 years?

4. **"E *Squared*" in Wildwood** – October 2014

Back in Florida, the young girl waiting on me at Barnes & Noble checked all over the state before declaring she would have to place an order for *The Midnight Fairies* and she would call me when it came in.

As I was hurrying to find the skinny guy, I spied a black book with bright yellow trim and picked it up. It was written by Pam Grout and titled *"E Squared"*[28]. After a quick glance at the back cover, I put it down. I picked up a few more books and then picked up Pam's book again and read a bit more. The book stated it was a "*lab manual with simple experiments that prove reality is malleable, consciousness trumps matter, and you shape your life with your mind*". It sounded way too scientific for me, so back it went on the shelf. Just then I saw the skinny guy waiting by the door, and with no further thought, I grabbed *E Squared* and headed directly to the checkout. Although it wouldn't be my usual reading choice, there seemed to be something about it that tweaked my curiosity. When I got home, I stuck it on the top of my pile of unread *books* and promptly forgot about it.

On a quiet November morning, after my husband left for an early round of golf, I decided to laze the morning away. While still in my fuzzy, blue bathrobe lazily sipping my coffee, I spied *"E Squared"* on the bookcase and opened to the first chapter.

Experiment #1 – *The Dude Abides Principle* was simple enough – "*ask any question you like, and the answer will come within seven days.*" Well, I had a great question because there was no way it could be answered, so I would immediately prove this book was a hoax. I followed the directions which were *"write down the question you wish to ask and then date it and wait up to seven days for an answer."*

I wrote:
Did my Father love me? November 30, 2014. At that moment a rusty ice chest opened its creaky door; and I felt the jagged icicles inside were being covered by a coating of molten honey— warmth and love was filling the space.

A flood of tears started rolling down my cheeks — *my father was killed on that day,*
November 30th exactly 55 years ago.

COSMIC MESSAGES: SYNCHRONICITY & COINCIDENCE

Synchronicity is a *pink* thread. The colour *pink* is symbolic of tenderness, love, sticky honey and sweetness.

Coincidence is a *bright yellow* thread (a positive coincidence). Bright yellow denotes a radiating sun, energy, happiness, intellect. I immediately thought of the cover of E *Squared*.

The coincidences and timing of the synchronicities involved in that *one* moment in time were beyond belief! My heart thawed! I was moved and started dancing around the living room led by an unknown feeling — a feeling of being guided and loved by my Father. Compassion and forgiveness would come later through the words of two gifted women.

My Cosmic Companions worked hard to orchestrate all those happenings that came together for one awe-inspiring moment. Now I could see my Cosmic Companions and my Father jumping up and down with glee that *their mission* had been accomplished!

A year and a half later, I knew, without a doubt, that this phenomenon was not by chance!

FRIDAY THE 13TH

A year later Friday, November 13, 2015, Bette, my mother-in-law of forty-six years, passed away.

Death smelled like money!

Bette could be a cold, vengeful woman. She also had a heart that was scared to show the love she felt. Through the years she nurtured her interest in astrology, numerology and palm reading – actually she became quite good at it until her vision became a problem.

At the age of 87 she was ready to meet her Maker. Dying on Friday the 13th would have made her day! Her nursing care attendants were disappointed that they would no longer have her in their care. She was definitely a challenge but her playful side won them over.

After she passed, I had a reading with Debra, the Medium[29], and Bette came through. She was indicating to Debra that she was cold. I explained that Bette always kept her feelings under wrap and did not show warmth to those she loved. Bette was nodding agreement; she conveyed to Debra she'd had a metamorphosis and now had a *renovated soul*. I was thrilled to hear this good news. Loved the term *renovated soul!*

Every week during her later life, Bette faithfully purchased lotto tickets, and she felt one hundred percent certain she would win a million dollars before she died. Unfortunately, that didn't happen. Seven months after her death, her firstborn grandchild won a dream house. The house was located in a community that bore the *family* name and, to top it off, behind the back fence was the family cemetery dating back to the 1700's.

I can picture our family Witch smiling and indicating she knew all along one of the family would win the million and I bet you anything she played a role in her grandchild's good fortune.

COSMIC MESSAGES: MAGIC & COINCIDENCE

The colour *orange* denotes magic! Joy, enthusiasm, happiness and new beginnings all rolled up together.

The colour *bright yellow* (a positive coincidence) denotes radiating sun, happiness and intellect

COSMIC COLOURS

CHAPTER SEVEN

PINK
COSMIC MESSAGE: SYNCHRONICITY - tenderness, love, sweetness

BRIGHT YELLOW
COSMIC EVENT: COINCIDENCE - positive coincidence, radiating sun, intellect and happiness

ORANGE
COSMIC COMPANION: WITCH - an ability to make magic happen

Chapter Eight

THE TRINITY

AND THEN THERE WERE THREE

I dreamed my sister, daughter and I were wearing blue dresses with flared skirts linked together by white sashes. We were flying over smooth, oval stones in an active, free-flowing brook that loudly and vigorously made its way to a river, then emptied into a sparkling, aqua ocean. Donna was leading the way, I was in the middle, and Amanda's sash trailed off into the air. The colours, the stones, the different forms of water and the fact we were flying left me feeling a sense of freedom and joy!

Flying, in dreams, is a form of astral projection where our soul leaves the body for a short time. Once we become aware of that state, we usually snap back into our body. "Call unto Me, and I will answer, and show thee great and mighty things, which thou knowest not." Jeremiah 33:3 NKJV. The words "Call on me, and I will answer," opened my eyes to the power of asking for what we want and need. It strengthened my belief that the Divine One hears our prayers. To interpret this dream was a test of perception and went hand in hand in developing an awareness of ordinary things (dreams and numbers, as symbols) that carry important messages and bring miracles into our life.

As you know from the chapter called *The Water Years,* the Cosmic Colour of a water dream is a blue thread representing healing and plumbing the depths to uncover our true emotions and free our trapped souls. Seeing the three forms of water in this dream, the brook, the river and ocean, reinforced the concept of a *trinity* joined on a mission to tell the stories of our ancestors.

> *A prayer by a single person has power; the prayer of a*
> *"Trinity" is immeasurable!*
> MargieGrams

Mindless Movement

cool grass under feet

legs bare, arms raised

hips sway gently

hesitantly softly

breath and heart

earth's rhythm

quickens with the wind

Leaves quiver, hair flies

faster, harsher

power and emotion

spill into darkness

from bone and blood

to roots and dirt

all are connected

indifferent moon above

witness to the dance

—*Donna L. Gray*[30]

COSMIC COMPANION: NUMBER 3:33 – THE TRINITY

This Cosmic Companion is a *white* thread. The colour of reverence and faith. Healing is tripled by three. This thread denotes a high level of awareness and is evident in those who *go beyond the norm* e.g. helping the ancestors move toward the light. The number *three* indicates the *Cosmic Door* is wide open to a Higher Power who is assisting us on our mission. The number *three* resonates with stopping the cycles of alcoholism, abuse and neglect. The prayer of *three* is tripled in intensity.

ANCESTORS

After reading *It Didn't Start with You,* [31] I felt: *my ancestors' energy being passed on to me and my relatives."* In other words, we were it!

As we arise and awake, awareness dawns. This is where change for the ancestors can occur. By our acknowledging what happened in the past and forgiving them their trespasses, healing occurs, and they sing and dance their way to the light. This *breaking the silence and voicing the secrets* is something only we can bring them. It is also the treasure for future generations. My lineage was from people who ran from what seemed to them unbearable circumstances. Alcohol and/

or substance abuse was the poison of choice. My father was a stretcher bearer in the war and I can hardly imagine the horrors he saw while carrying soldiers off the battlefield. When I realize the lengths, he went to to connect with me, the importance of having compassion and forgiveness is monumental. There also seems to be a history of infant loss in our family. By bringing the misery of past generations into the light, healing can begin. Quite the burden! If we shy away from this task, the pain and suffering keeps on happening. No pressure!

Whispers

We'll take our souls
For a stroll
Through the birches
The trees of new beginnings.
Tune into the rhythm of life,
Listen for the sounds of creation,
Hear the soft whispers
Of the ancients thanking us
As they head to the light
While we prepare
For new patterns of living.

—MargieGrams

COSMIC COLOURS

CHAPTER EIGHT

WHITE
COSMIC MESSAGE: NUMBER 3:33 THE TRINITY - Jeremiah 3:33 - prayers are heard and answered - expect to see great and mighty things. The power of three people praying for the same thing is immeasurable.

Chapter Nine

THE THREE GIFTS

ANOTHER MOTHER'S DAY 2017

The previous year, Mother's Day 2016, we were driving back from our daughter and son-in-law's home after the loss of Nathaniel Xavier. This Mother's Day the skinny guy gifted me and my daughter airline tickets to visit my two sisters, Donna and Deanne, on Vancouver Island. He generously offered to fly with me to our daughter's in Ontario to help our son-in-law with the grandkids while my daughter and I took a much-needed trip out west. I had spent the last six months writing and a break was just what I needed. My daughter was overjoyed to get to spend time with me and her aunts.

TRIP OUT WEST

Donna was very excited we were coming and surprised Amanda, Deanne and me with a spiritual reading with her good friend, a well-respected Spiritual Medium named Debra Doerksen who lived in the area. The day of the reading dawned bright and sunny as we arrived at Debra's. Debra's friend, Diana, also a Medium, ushered us into a private room for readings and once we sat down, they both said a prayer for guidance and protection. After a quiet period, Debra started describing a cat identical in size and colour to Freya. My daughter and I shared a smile. Debra told me she was one of my spirit animals who helped heal my sore throat when I was in Florida. All I could think of is no one in that room ever knew of my experience of seeing Freya outside my window in Wildwood mainly because I never trusted my intuition or had enough faith to believe it really could have been Freya. This blew my mind!

Debra intuited a message from my late father, where she described his stature and saw him standing with his hands behind his back. She felt his message was *his hands were tied*. She asked me if I had any idea what he was trying to tell me. Of course, I immediately thought of the rough period we all went through when my mother left him in June 1959. He seemed to be indicating that my mother wouldn't give him any more chances and wouldn't take him back. Then he showed Debra what looked like a plush snake. When she asked me if that had any meaning, all I could think of was in Florida we were warned not to garden in the spring without long pants secured at the ankle as the snakes in the grass were poisonous. Then it hit me! After many unwelcome appearances at my aunt's home, where we were staying, one day the police had to be called as he cut and tore up what little clothes my Mom had. Of course, he acted *like a snake in the grass! Now he was taking responsibility for his despicable actions.*

Debra then saw him, walking the perimeter, with a rifle in his hands. Being in the army, he had owned and used rifles, of course. He was indicating to Debra that *he was walking the perimeter to protect me.* As I was absorbing this reading, I was envisioning my father in his army uniform and I felt a softening of my heart. Was he actually trying to convince me of his remorse and let me know he would protect me now—would it be possible to truly forgive this man?

Just then, Debra moved quietly from her chair to her bookcase and, with no hesitation, picked a slim book off the shelf and sat down. With a slight smile, she told me my father wanted me to have this particular book. She said sometimes a spirit will request she read a certain part, but my father wanted me to have the entire book. She gave me *The Dance of the Mystic Healer*[32] by Eileen Curteis. I flipped to the back of the book and read:

Sister Eileen composed a volume of song-verses or singable ballads in the process of her spiritual journey into joy and health. Her uplifting poetry of the often painful and poignant trials of life bring hope that there is a purpose after all. We have only in the words of Joseph Campbell to "follow our bliss" in order to find it. I sat there stunned.

This book was written by a nun who had suffered the trials of life but had searched for and found compassion in her heart. For some reason, this fact impacted me greatly. Here are a few stanzas that Sister Eileen permitted me to use:

Road of Compassion

A haphazard jigsaw
Scattered on the floor
I'm a blind woman walking
Who is healing to the core

Squashing all my feelings
They've become like stinging bees
And the hurricane inside me
Is uprooting every tree.
No longer living in silence

With my mouth inside a sling
I'm repairing all the damage
This kind of violence brings…
—Eileen Curteis[33]

Once back in Nova Scotia, I contacted Sister Eileen Curteis and after an e-mail connection, she arranged to speak with me, so I could tell her my story of how the book was gifted to me, through Debra, by my late father. Nothing I told her shocked or surprised. She graciously took it all in stride. Eileen Curteis has a new book called *EXPOSED* which I am looking forward to reading.

COSMIC COMPANION: BOOK - SISTER EILEEN CURTEIS

This Cosmic Companion is a *gold* thread.

The colour gold signifies wisdom, endurance, courage and confidence. The author's healing journey lifted and inspired me. Our conversation surrounding this gift of her book left me in awe of the powers of our Cosmic Companions.

The Dance of the Mystic Healer and how I came to have it was a miracle. The most amazing thing was having a telephone conversation with the author on the other side of the country to tell her that my father, who at that time had been deceased for 57 years, gifted me her book.

COSMIC COMPANION: A MEDIUM

This Cosmic Companion is an *indigo* and a *violet* thread.

Indigo denotes intuition and psychic ability. Violet denotes an ability to open a doorway to spirit. Debra has a *higher cosmic consciousness* which enables her to open the *cosmic door* and connect with spirit.

COSMIC IMPS

Back in Wildwood and working diligently on my writing, I logged on and went to *Word* to check the last few pages I typed the day before, and they were nowhere to be found. After quite a search, I accepted defeat and started rewriting my reading from Debra in June. When I got to the part where Debra hands me the book, instead of typing the book name I turned on the dictation microphone. I clearly pronounced the words *The Dance* and when I checked it had printed out the word *Daughter*. *Daughter*, where in the heck did that come from? I turned off the microphone, and then turned it back on thinking I had done something strange; and, with extra attention to the pronunciation, I clearly repeated *THE DANCE*. When I glanced at the iPad, I could barely believe what I saw:

Gotcha, Gotcha!

I was creeped out, incredulous and then I started to laugh –today was November 30, 2017–the 58th anniversary of my Father's death. Can you believe it? Now he's being funny!

With God all things are possible.
Matthew 19:26

COSMIC COLOURS

CHAPTER NINE

GOLD
COSMIC COMPANION: BOOK - SISTER EILEEN CURTEIS - spirituality on a supreme level; deep connection with wisdom, solitude and clairvoyance

INDIGO AND VIOLET
COSMIC COMPANION: THE MEDIUM - ability to open a doorway to a higher consciousness and connect with spirit

Chapter Ten

SONG AND DANCE

TOUCH MY SOUL

Still relishing memories from my trip out west, my husband and I took a car ride to visit our good friends, Bob and Olive.

I dug out a book to read on the way published by Francine Shapiro called *When the Past is Present*[34]. I opened randomly to a page entitled *Finding the Touchstone Memories* and started reading. Francine explains that *the earliest unprocessed memory that sets the groundwork for a particular problem is called a Touchstone Memory. . . ones that are hot, the ones that are negative and can be a single event, such as a major trauma that would form the basis for PTSD…*

She went on to explain how *veterans of war were quoted explaining how one minute they are loving to their family and then they turn on them.* Back in the 50's when my Father was in the Korean War, PTSD was unheard of. Aunt Gloria in 2014 was trying to convince me my Father suffered from PTSD.

Just then, a song came on Siri and I glanced up—the time was 11:11 a.m. and I just caught the name — *Touch Me* by *The Doors!* Okay, my cosmic companions I'm ready and connected to receive *the messages I need to hear.* I checked out the number 11:11 in the New American Bible - Luke 11:11 - "What Father are you who hands his son a snake when he asks for a fish?" I went completely quiet when I read this and felt that my father couldn't be any clearer in trying to communicate his love for me. This Cosmic Message is definitely a white coloured thread!

My strong feelings about no doors, locked doors, closed doors kept nagging at me. I decided to check out *The Doors,* a band popular in the 60's, to see if anything resonated with me. *The Doors* were an American Rock Band formed in 1965, in Los Angeles, with vocalist Jim Morrison, keyboardist Ray Manzarek, guitarist Robby Krieger, and John Densmore on drums. The band got its name, at Morrison's suggestion from the title of Aldous Huxley's book *The Doors of Perception,* which itself was a reference to a quote made by William Blake*:*

> *"If the doors of perception were cleansed, everything would appear to man as it is, infinite. For man has closed himself up, till he sees all things thru' narrow chinks of his cavern."*
>
> — *William Blake, The Marriage of Heaven and Hell*[35]

After a pregnant pause, I continued reading, and, I kid you not, I opened randomly to the subtitle *The Snake in the Grass.* This coincidence couldn't be any clearer. My Father, in the reading showed Debra what looked like a plush snake. I deduced he was apologizing for acting like a snake in the grass when they separated. Evidently my cosmic helpers were pulling out all the stops to make sure I clearly understood my father's message. I couldn't wait to share this new coincidence with my sister and daughter. What are the odds?

COSMIC MESSAGE: MUSIC

The coloured thread for music is a *silver* thread which denotes imagination.

Music is smooth, pure and conveys feelings. It spoke for my soul when I didn't have the courage to put my feelings into words and speak them out loud. It allowed me to stay safe while I dipped my toe in the water of my truth.

> *After silence, that which comes nearest to expressing the inexpressible is music.* —Aldous Huxley[36]

COSMIC MESSAGE: COINCIDENCE

The coloured thread for coincidence is *yellow* which helps with inner vision, confidence, communication and is like the sun radiating clarity. This message solidified for me my Aunt Gloria's belief that my Father had been suffering from PTSD. I finally "got it"!

IS THAT YOU MOM?

Late August, my daughter and her family's summer visit was coming to an end. Lots of thoughts were going through my head. When would we see them next? How much we had enjoyed having them close for the last ten days. How much we would miss their lively presence.

Before she left, my daughter laid a box in my lap and when I opened it, I saw it was a beautiful scallop shell, hand-painted with a gorgeous blue jay. My daughter saw it while shopping for souvenirs to take back to Toronto and she couldn't resist buying it for me. It brought back a positive memory of my mother who loved keeping watch on a blue jay nest in the tree outside her 4th floor apartment window. I will never forget how excited she was when she called me at work to tell me the baby blue jays hatched.

After Mom's death, when I saw a blue jay, I would comment to whoever I was with *there goes Mom*. As my friends' mothers passed away, I encouraged them to imagine my Mom welcoming theirs into what I called *The Bluejay Club*.

Coincidentally, that very same afternoon, my son found a blue jay feather in his backyard and gave it to me. My mother and this son had a very close bond as he was the first grandson. This was the first time I had ever seen a blue jay feather up close, and I was astounded by its beautiful colours – how the shades of blues and blacks complemented each other. The very next day, while on the golf course, my husband found a blue jay feather and brought it home to me. Mom was desperately trying to get my attention as she watched from above and I'm guessing she wanted to let me know she approved of the change in my feelings for my father. The blue jay has a passion for investigation, thus allowing us to access memories that we have long forgotten and shows us how to adopt them into our awareness. Wow, this was spot on!

> A blue jay [37] flies into your life to teach the importance of using your intelligence to learn and adapt quickly to any situation. The blue jay has mastered the balance between patience and silence. This allows it to develop a deep connection with the Earth, uncovering sacred interconnections between all things.

I like to think my Mom was letting me know she was around and delighted that her only granddaughter was assisting her as she worked with the cosmic companions to solidify the messages I was getting.

COSMIC COMPANION: BLUE JAY

This Cosmic Companion is a *pink* thread. Pink is symbolic of the heart chakra — sweetness and love.

Blue jays love to use their voices to chatter back and forth as did my mother. She loved nothing better than to regale a group of her girlfriends with funny stories and hear their peals of laughter. I like to picture her dipping a feather in ink as she wrote the following poem.

Looking Out to Sea

One small boy on a lonely shore
Gazing out to sea
Picturing in his mind's eye
What a sailor's life must be.

To cross the oceans wide and blue
With foreign ports of call
Be captain of a sailing ship
Would be the greatest thrill of all.

To feel the sea spray on my face
To hear the wind's wild roar
To watch the crimson sun set
Could a sailor ask for more?
When I grow to be a man
One day perhaps I'll see
That all I dream of on the shore
Will come to pass for me.

—Florence Eliza (Baldwin) (Davies) Gray (deceased 1986)

THE DANCE OF LIFE

> *Life is like a dance, it all flows beautifully until we are thrown up in the air and there's no one to catch us.*
>
> —*MargieGrams*

When I look back on my life, I see what I call the six S's:

Suffering – The first ten years – *Life with the Villain*
Survival – The next twenty years –
It was the Best of Times: It was the Worst of Times
Silence & Seeking – The next thirty plus years – *The Water Years*
Surrender & Sharing – 2014 – the present – *The Catalysts*

Song of Suffering:

I can't help but think that I had an upbringing that would have been common to a great many people, especially those born in the forties, fifties and sixties. I am just one of the *walking wounded*. Paul Levy[38] writes "*it is only by being willing to face, consciously experience, and go through our wound do we receive its blessing*". It seemed to ring true that only by exposing the wound to the air, could it start to heal. Exploring the trauma of my past, through writing, pushed my ego out of the way so I could dig deep and face the truth of my younger years.

Song of Survival:

If I was to make up a song title for these years it would be *Swimming in the Rain*.

Song of Silence and Seeking:

> *Ask, and it will be given to you; seek and you will find; knock, and it will be opened to you. For everyone who asks receives, and he who seeks finds, and to him who knocks it will be opened.*
>
> —Matthew 7:7-8NKJV

I learned to set boundaries and to find some *me time*. I woke up and realized that I was responsible for my own happiness. I was my own worst enemy. I needed to refill my bucket—no one could do this for me.

I knocked on every door and left no stone unturned on my mission to find me. My morning reading had a lovely line:

> *Trust in me wholeheartedly, beloved, for I am your strength and your song.*
> — Isaiah 12:2

Song of Surrender and Sharing:

I clearly remember dropping my Great-Grandmother's platter and the large crack that ensued. I now realize that the cracks show us what we need to learn about ourselves.

I was totally devastated when this happened. It was as if I had broken the link with my ancestors. It made me feel sad and bereft not to see that platter in my glassed-in cabinet.

My dear friend, Olive, shared the last lines in one of her favourite novels and it resonated with me in a big way:

The last line in *Niko,* a novel by Dimitri Nasrallah,[39] clearly speaks to me:

> *That is why people are designed to carry mistakes,*
> *and this is why people should keep a room in their souls*
> *for what they might have done differently.*

At first, the idea of *a room in my soul* provided me with a scary visual. As I opened that door it was loaded with pots wedged among huge boulders; I saw my mother trying to get back on her feet after she was pushed and fell among the dolls and trucks in our toy box; a homemade hutch was lying on the floor surrounded by broken shards of glass and cracked dishes. The time had come to renovate my soul room!

It was evident from my recent experiences, my father had enlisted all the cosmic companions he could muster up to show his remorse and make amends. He had to rid himself of his rocks of regret and stones of sorrow to move toward the light. His messages rang true with me and I felt it was time now for me to move forward as well!

Now my *soul room* is filled with music, blue jays are flitting from birch to oak trees as the grandchildren laugh, play and curl up on my lap for snuggles. My hope and joy is they will go forward free of the baggage of their ancestors.

During the *Water Years* I had no desire to redecorate anything, I wish I'd known then I had a *"soul room"!*

Sodalite

Cold, Blue, Stone of Truth
Release the bonds of silence
That fear has wrapped
around my soul.

The truth inside me released
With quiet strength
I find my voice
In the middle of my thoughts and feelings

My heart sings freedom
Arms raised to the night
I dance with my tears
Under a cold, blue, sky

—Donna L. Gray[40]

COSMIC COLOURS

CHAPTER TEN

PINK
COSMIC COMPANION: BIRD (BLUE JAY) - tenderness, sweetness – a balance between the spiritual and earth realm using voice and silence

SILVER
COSMIC MESSAGE: MUSIC - imagination; gives voice to the inexpressible feelings

YELLOW
COSMIC MESSAGE: COINCIDENCE - positive coincidence, an attention getter, joy, intellect and happiness.

WHITE
COSMIC MESSAGE: NUMBER 11:11 denotes the heavens are trying to communicate. Pay attenion.

Chapter Eleven

I'm Grounded

A SETBACK – September 2017

Family vacation was over — time to get on with my everyday life. I was preparing a two-session bridge workshop for 24 students with a light lunch included. As the day approached I was experiencing sciatica pain down my left leg which I attributed to the extra stairs and activity of the family holiday. I did my usual icing, meds and floor exercises but after the full day of teaching, I experienced leg and foot pain that was excruciating. It was time to go to the professionals for help.

A herniated disc with a fragment in the nerve root side-lined me for nine months. I got the message loud and clear from my body that my activity level was about to come to a standstill. No golfing for me, shopping was impossible, as well as anything to do with cooking and cleaning (now that part wasn't too hard to take). The *skinny guy* stepped up to the plate and earned a place in the *Husband Hall of Fame*. As I was thrown into the air, he caught me and developed something I never thought I would see—patience!

The Universe opened wide for me in a spiritual way. I had *me time*!

I SAT – I WROTE

—while I waited for a date with the surgeon.

SMOKE AND CEREMONY

In this vivid dream, I saw large round holes cut in the earth leaving green swaths of grass surrounding the holes. There was smoke rising from the holes. According to Pamela Ball, *"10,000 Dreams Explained"*, [41]

> A round hole traditionally represents the heavens – any hole that allows steam or smoke to escape is an opening upwards to the celestial world or prayer rising heavenward.

At this time in my life, I was giving thanks to everyone who rallied round to support me. I was also praying for a miracle to get the surgery date sooner than later. By the way, I got that miracle courtesy of my Cosmic Doctor!

Also, in this dream there was a clock set at 1:11. In my dream it signaled the time had come to have a *tea ceremony*. A tea ceremony, how wonderful! Our bridge group once arrived in kimonos (disguised bathrobes) with chopsticks stuck in their hair, carrying fans in case of a hot flash. Sue was about to travel to Japan for work, so we thought we would have a tea ceremony to guarantee her safe travels.

COSMIC MESSAGE: SMOKE

This cosmic message will be a *gray* thread. The colour gray opens us to possibilities and interpretations—things can be blurry. Smoke in dreams can represent giving thanks.

COSMIC MESSAGE: DREAM – NUMBER -1:11

This Cosmic Messenger 1:11 is an auspicious sign. A *brown* thread signifying a call to raise my vibration.

- Time to solidify the messages from my Cosmic Companions and focus on forgiveness and compassion
- Time to release my prayers and thanks to the heavens for my cosmic helpers
- Time to work on my life purpose and watch the universe reveal the tapestry

Time, such a precious gift – time to just *be!* Time was the silver lining.

COSMIC COLOURS

CHAPTER ELEVEN

GRAY
COSMIC MESSAGE: DREAM: SMOKE - open to possibilities and interpretations; things can be blurry

BROWN
COSMIC COMPANION: NUMBER 1:11 – time to raise my vibration;
And to appreciate the value of ceremonies and rituals

Chapter Twelve

Destiny's Dreams

ENDINGS AND BEGINNINGS

My surgery was a success, and within a few weeks we flew back to Wildwood. I was full of joy and thankfulness for all my doctors, surgeons, husband, family and special friends who went to bat for me and supported me during this difficult time.

Sitting in our Florida lanai, I couldn't help but be awed at the wonder all around me. This room would qualify as a *renovated soul room*! The rain moved on and the atmosphere felt like a warm, milk bath— creamy and languid. The Spanish moss hanging from the oak trees was catching the late afternoon breeze and there was just a hint of air caressing it as it clutched the sturdy oaks. Oh, what wisdom could be found if I had Merlin's key to the door to the oak trees —*the keepers of greatest knowledge and wisdom, as well as one's ancestral memory...*

The grass was a vivid, almost iridescent green. I heard a clatter as an acorn dropped onto the tin roof and just barely caught sight of a rambunctious squirrel sliding down the drain spout. A citrus-coloured golf cart whizzed by and the owner's Golden Retriever sat up proudly in the passenger seat eager for his afternoon trip to the dog run.

My mind reached back for a moment to my need to have a door to my bedroom. I now know that I was seeking *to be sheltered* from the pain and trauma of living with an abusive parent. The fact that my father was suffering and in pain does not negate his behaviour. However, it made me think of a book I read as a teenager about reincarnation that made a huge impact on my life. There was a scenario that I've never forgotten, that could shed a different light on my father's role. I will describe my interpretation for you:

I visualized my father and me, before we came to earth this time round, discussing the ancestors who were waiting patiently in the afterlife for healing of past traumas they caused. Could it be possible that before we both were born into this current life, we loved each other dearly, and we agreed to share a life on earth where he would play the neglectful, abusive father and I would play the traumatized daughter in hopes of accomplishing ancestral healing. Once he completed his part of the arrangement, he died. Now, the ball was in my court! Could I *awaken* from this *dream of life,* and carry out the mission!

I lived a full, ordinary life before our family crisis forced me to deal with my past trauma. Once I reached that point, a door opened and sent me lots of helpers. I can only imagine the cheering and tumbling taking place when I finally woke up to what I needed to do. During my personal journey to heal, I was literally forced to look back to the past. This healing journey involved being open to receive and accept the messages my father sent that he loved me and was remorseful for the pain he caused. As I dug deep in my heart, forgiveness and compassion surfaced and closed an open wound and a chapter in my life.

I put together the coloured threads of my cosmic companions and the universe revealed the tapestry that led me to the answers I had been seeking since I was ten years old: What am I here for? It was as if I remembered my part of the pact and knew, without a doubt, I was here, along with my sister and daughter to heal the past, so my father and the ancestors could move toward the light. Future generations will no longer have to linger in the dark. A fresh start – *a new beginning for our family*. A bonus—in doing so I also healed myself.

> You are a link in a chain of causation that stretches before and after your life for a thousand generations.
> —Rev. Chris Michaels[42], founding minister of the Center for Spiritual Living, Kansas City, Missouri

THE DAY

I took a sip of my ice-cold water and, now rejuvenated, returned to reading *The Healing Power of Trees*.[43] While I was visiting my sister in British Columbia in June 2017, this book was sitting on the bookshelf. I opened it and began reading and it was if this book mesmerized me. Donna, seeing how absorbed I was in the book, gave it to me to take home to Nova Scotia.

Incidentally, the powerful dreams I had—the Druids, the Quote and the Denuded Birch all took place in the fall of 2016 before I discovered this book.

Sharlyn HiDalgo's quote spoke directly to me:

> *"Samhain is called The Day and is the most important celebration of the year... It's meaning are endings and beginnings, and death and rebirth."*

Ironically, this celebration called "The Day" begins at sunset on my birthday, *October 30*, and extends into the Celtic New Year which begins at sunset of October 31st. My life was certainly about *endings* and *new beginnings, death and rebirth*. The fact that the *birch* is the tree of the Celtic New Year is like icing on the cake! Ah, there was a primal reason I was drawn to birch trees in my dreams and in my life. As I sat quietly in deep thought, the sky darkened, and a shower left glistening raindrops on the awning. I was fascinated by a tiny drop clinging to the edge for dear life.

I jotted down the following…

Destiny's Dreams

By exploring the past
I've found answers at last
That helpless little girl
Who was scared as she could be
Has now been held and rocked
By the strong woman who is me
I learn patience as I walk
My path
In my own time
And listen to the whispers of the birches
As they reveal my destiny
—MargieGrams

Now I look to the future and, as I face the aspect of aging and all that comes with that phase of life, I need all the strength, courage and compassion I can muster up. I am confident that with the help of my Cosmic Companions, I will keep on my path to the light of a Higher Power. My sister wrote a poem that I think embodies what we were called to do together in this lifetime:

FIRE

Embrace the dark and broken pieces of your soul
Your strength is born of the scars and the
Fire that burns and shapes, burns and shapes.
Dance among the flames until nothing remains

But the warm grey ash of who you once were.
In your heart are the embers of the ones who danced before you
The oceans are filled, and the earth is cleansed
With their tears of sorrow and joy.
Let go, release yourself to the wind and trust, just trust
Love and dreams are carried through the air
And the sun shines fresh light upon the earth
Dance new spirit, fast, strong and full of heat
On this path forged from the fires of us all

—Donna L. Gray[44]

My cosmic cheerleaders were dancing, singing and showering me with feathers; and

I could see my ancestors walking one by one as they gleefully headed towards the *Cosmic Door* and the *Light*.

Conclusion

The Three Big - A's

In one of my dreams in 2014, during the time of the midnight fairy coincidences and synchronicities, I had a dream of three words printed in large letters on a piece of paper. The words were: awake, accept and aware. To be perfectly honest I dismissed them as *just words*. I smile now as I realize how much work my Cosmic Companions had to undertake to *awaken* me to *acceptance*. At that time, I was sadly lacking *awareness!*

By choosing *acceptance* of *what is,* relinquishing control and surrendering to a Higher Power, I opened the Cosmic Door. I no longer felt the compulsive urge to search. The Universe then responded by flooding my life with enthusiastic helpers who did everything in their power to help me *awaken* to the fact that I was put here for a purpose I had long ago forgotten. I now had found my purpose and it all made perfect sense. All it took was *awareness*!

What was my father's message?

My father enlisted a troop of Cosmic Companions, who orchestrated experiences and events, to give me his messages that he took responsibility and was remorseful for his behaviour. Now he was walking the perimeter to protect me.

What was going on with me and doors?

I started out having no doors to protect me. Then at age ten, I locked the door to my heart. The crisis in 2016 precipitated the unlocking of the door to my *broken heart.* Our road trip to see Bob and Olive comes to mind and my bewilderment over the music of *The Doors* and that nagging feeling that there was something I wasn't getting. Finding out that the word for *oak* is *duir* which also means *door* tied up some loose ends. *Merlin* the *Oak Knower,* who held the key to the wisdom of the ancients worked diligently for years to keep me on my journey to find my destiny. The Cosmos showered me with Cosmic Companions to help me find the answers I needed to why I was here.

Am I still a seeker?

The answer is *No.* I realize now I was a "relentless seeker." Each new book I bought promised an answer to why I was here on this earth. When I finally woke up to the messages in dreams, symbols, music, nature, animals and people, I was awestruck. I had been so busy looking outside myself, I missed what was staring me in the face. Now I quietly and calmly observe and process my life experiences—the answers are to be found there.

What am I here for?

> *Some people are here for the past*
> *Some people are here for the future*

I am here for the past—to forgive my father so he can move to the light and take all our ancestors with him.

Did death shape me?

The answer is *no*! Life shaped me! Through this process I have learned to ask my Cosmic Companions for help and guidance, to trust in a Higher Power, and to be *grateful* every day for big and small mercies. I love how George Bernard Shaw[45] put it:

> **Life is no 'brief candle' for me. It is a sort of splendid torch which I have got hold of for the moment, and I want to make it burn as brightly as possible before handing it on to future generations.**

Once you become *aware*, there is no going back
—just a *simple awareness* is all it takes!

*We delight in the beauty of the butterfly,
But rarely admit the changes it has gone thru
To achieve that state. A.U.*

Life

*Life, believe, is not a dream
So dark as sages say;
Oft a little morning rain
Foretells a pleasant day.
Sometimes there are clouds of gloom,
But these are transient all;
If the shower will make the roses bloom,
O why lament its fall?
Rapidly, merrily,
Life's sunny hours flit by,
Gratefully, cheerily,
Enjoy them as they fly!
What though Death at times steps in,*

And calls our Best away?
What though sorrow seems to win,
O'er hope, a heavy sway?
Yet hope again elastic springs,
Unconquered, though she fell;
Still buoyant are her golden wings,
Still strong to bear us well.
Manfully, fearlessly,
The day of trial bear,
For gloriously, victoriously,
Can courage quell despair!
—Charlotte Bronte[46]

Appendix A

THE COSMIC COMPANIONS, EVENTS AND MESSAGES

START YOUR OWN EXPLORING

You need to claim the events of your life to make yourself yours.
Anne-Wilson Schaefer[47]

Each event in your life when held to the light, examined closely, and seen in context with every other experience, points you toward your destiny. To start your exploration, get a spiral notebook with a separate tabbed section and a pen.

On the first page of your notebook:

- Name the earliest life event or experience and that stood out for you

- Write down your age and the date it happened

- Was there anything unusual that you can recall before, during or after the event

COSMIC COMPANIONS, EVENTS AND MESSAGES

BLUE JAY
BOOK
CAT (Freya)
COINCIDENCE (POSITIVE)
COINCIDENCE (NEGATIVE)
COINCIDENCE (NEUTRAL)
DEATH
DENUDED BIRCH
DOORS
EARTH ANGEL
FATE/DESTINY
FEATHER
INFANT LOSS
MAGIC
MEDIUM
MUSIC
NUMBER 11:11
NUMBER: 1:11
NUMBER 3:33
OWL
PREMONITION
QUOTE
SMOKE
STONES
SYNCHRONICITY
TREES – BIRCH
WATER
WITCH
WIZARD

WHAT THEY DO:

- make you smile
- inspire you
- heal you
- inform you
- warn you
- wake you up
- nudge you
- urge you
- surprise you
- send you answers
- work with you to solve a conundrum
- cheer you
- dance, somersault and tumble to celebrate you
- choose music for you
- choose poems for you
- choose quotes for you
- choose people to come into your life
- protect you
- cry & shout with you

Appendix B

COSMIC COLOURS AND MEANINGS

BLACK – DEATH
BLUE – WATER
BROWN – CAT -TOTEM & COMPANION
BROWN – NUMBER 1:11
CHARCOAL – INFANT LOSS
GOLD – BOOK
GOLD – OWL
GRAY – SMOKE
GREEN – TREES (BIRCH)
GREEN – FEATHER
INDIGO – DOORS – DREAM
INDIGO – DENUDED BIRCH TREE
INDIGO – MEDIUM
ORANGE – MAGIC
ORANGE – WITCH
ORANGE – WIZARD
PINK – BLUE JAY
PINK – SYNCHRONICITY
PURPLE – STONES
PURPLE – QUOTE – DREAM
RED – FATE/DESTINY
SILVER – MUSIC

VIOLET – PREMONITION
WHITE – EARTH ANGELS
WHITE - NUMBER 11:11
WHITE – NUMBER 3:33
YELLOW (BRIGHT) – COINCIDENCE (POSITIVE)
YELLOW (DULL) – COINCIDENCE (NEGATIVE)
YELLOW – COINCIDENCE (NEUTRAL)

The meanings of the colours were chosen based on the feelings aroused from the cosmic companion, event, or experience. You may have a different colour that resonates with you, so please choose whatever colour works for you. If it is a colour not listed, you can choose any colour you like, and the meaning will come.

1. Write down the name of cosmic companion, message or event that you experienced
2. Write down the colour

At the end of this exercise, by weaving the texture and colour of your threads from each sign and message, you will have shaped the fabric of your life. You will glimpse your journey in a new light as you continue on your way to the Cosmic Door that opens to a Higher Consciousness.

BLACK is perfect because it is not a colour. When you are in mourning or darkness, you feel colourless. A black object absorbs all the colours and reflects none of them to the eyes. Beginnings and endings —change. Black is a dignified colour!

BLUE signifies exploring what's under the surface —digging deep into our subconscious —blue can soothe the soul. If you feel blue – sadness, depression and turmoil can reign.

BROWN is the colour that is calling you to raise your vibration.

- Time to search and find messages from spirit; Time to release prayers and thanks to the heavens for the cosmic helpers; Time to work on life purpose and watch the universe reveal the tapestry.

CHARCOAL is representative of a *dark gray* colour. The first recorded use of *charcoal as a colour* in England was 1606. This colour has a low vibration and is associated with a loss of light; a loss of words.

GOLD denotes the Midas touch, the top of the line, clairvoyance, gold stars for opportunities of greatness, the richness of life, attaining lofty goals

GRAY a blurring of lines, an in-between state.

GREEN is a nature colour and involves aliveness, budding, growth, and renewal. Nature's colours work together to claim you, calm you and restore you.

INDIGO this dark blue colour denotes cosmic consciousness – fulfillment of healing mind, body and spirit. An ability to open the *Cosmic Door* to a Higher Power.

ORANGE is a hot colour – joy, radiating sunshine, enthusiasm, and creativity all encompass the colour orange. Magic can happen!

PINK is symbolic of the heart—tenderness, love and sweetness.

PURPLE the colour of royalty, nobility, reaching great heights as in astral travel. Also, this colour speaks to extravagance, ceremonies, enlightenment and wisdom of the ages.

RED signifies desire, intensity, love and high energy.

SILVER wealth, sophistication, imagination.

VIOLET denotes the psychic power of premonition —foreboding and unconscious knowing. Intuition is a sense that comes *out of nowhere* and would be a perfect descriptor of my experience on November 30th, 1959.

WHITE is associated with contact with Higher Power, purity, love and healing.
Pay attention when you see 11:11 – the heavens are trying to communicate.

YELLOW (DULL) denotes a negative coincidence, caution – low vibrations.

YELLOW (VIBRANT) radiates like the sun – bright yellow denotes clarity, positivity, and stands out.

YELLOW (NEUTRAL) in general is a cheery, joyful colour...

Acknowledgments

Big hugs to the "skinny guy" who trucked out to buy me paper and ink cartridges at a moment's notice; complained only mildly when we moved from one country to another with a trunk filled with files and books, and surprised me with a futuristic lamp for my new desk. This book is written for my sons and daughter-in-law —Craig and Rochelle, Cori and Perri-Ann, my son-in-law, Marcel. My Cosmic Daughter, Amanda, what can I say, other than thanks for picking up the phone when you saw my number up. I was usually in a panic over something I did on Facebook, like downloading 250 pictures from an album of a bride I didn't know. Your love, encouragement, humour and words of wisdom have been a huge support. My sister, Deanne and nephew, Dakota, my late brother, Jack and nephew John. A huge embrace to my sister, Donna Gray, in Sooke, BC for writing her amazing poems that suited my book so eloquently. Donna, tripped over a sandwich board on a sidewalk in Victoria, BC. It happened to be "Tellwell Talent"! Thanks Mitch, Simon and the hard-working staff—although I can't deny Octavo and I have a few issues! Thank you to Aunt Gloria for putting in a good word for my father and answering all my questions. Thank you, cousin, Joan for your encouragement and enthusiasm as I started my writing journey. Love you and thank you all for sharing this life with me.

Thank you to my *Cosmic Techno Wizards*— Kevin Webber, Dick Arnold, Natalie Robbins and my techie friend, Susan Lundquist. Without these kind, talented, patient people, I would have ended up in "Word" hell! Thank you to my *Cosmic English Majors* —Olive Corning, Gayle Hancock, Susan Lundquist and Carol Stevens Hale for checking my manuscript for flow, grammar, punctuation, spelling and run on sentences. Carol and I worked side-by-side as Legal Secretaries, off and on, from 1974 to 1995 (lots of proofreading talent there)! Carol was the first one who told me *I should write a book!*

About The Author

MARGARET JOLLIMORE

www.MargieGrams.com

Born in Halifax NS, Margaret and her husband, Brad, also lived in New Glasgow & Sydney, NS; Burnaby & Vancouver, BC; Ottawa & Kingston, ON and St. John's, NL. They currently divide their time between Halifax, NS and Wildwood, Fl.

Margaret's passion is teaching bridge. When Margaret retired as a legal secretary, she obtained a Certificate in Adult Education; along with an ACBL Bridge Teacher Accreditation. She would like Oprah to know she would love to teach her and her friends how to play this amazing game. It would be lots of fun on a cruise ship. Margaret and Merlin go way back and she believes it when Merlin says: "learning something new is the key to successful aging." - www.thebridgeguru.com

Margaret's favourite dessert is anything with caramel in or on it!

Endnotes

1. W Yeats, W.B. – Quote
2. Woolf, Virginia – Quote
3. Richard Maurice Burke, Cosmic Consciousness: A Study in the Evolution of the Human Mind, (Canada, 1900 – Innes & Sons, 1311 Sansom St. Philadelphia, 1905 ED)
4. Ranier Maria Rilke – Quote (Died Dec. 29, 1926)
5. Emily Elizabeth Dickinson, Hope, (Public Domain, 1830-1886) – Wikisource.org/wiki/Poems: Second Series
6. Donna L. Gray, Reaction, (Sooke, BC, 2017)
7. Johnson, Barbara – Quote
8. Donna L. Gray, Breathe, (Sooke, BC, 2017)
9. Nora Chadwick, The Celts, The Druids, (University of Wales Press, 1966)
10. Sharlyn HiDalgo, The Healing Power of Trees (Llewllyn, MN, 2011) p.26 & 28
11. Genetic memory (psychology) Wikipedia
12. T.H. White, The Once and Future King, Subject: Merlin on Aging, collected and published shorter novels 1938-1941 - Wikipedia
13. Pamela Ball, 10,000 Dreams Explained, (London, UK, Arcturus Publishing, 2015)
14. Lolo Morganwg, Welsh Poet; cy:wikisource:Gweddi'r Orsedd

15 Donna L, Gray – opinion on "The Quote"
16 Mark Wolynn, It Didn't Start with You, (Viking, An Imprint of Penguin, Random House LLC, 2016)
17 Albert Einstein- Quote
18 Sharlyn HiDalgo, The Healing Power of Trees (Llewllyn, MN, 2011)
19 Freya, Norse Goddess – Wikipedia
20 Geoffrey of Monmouth – The History of Kings of Britain (1136) – historical information presented by Wikipedia (adapted and translated,e.g., by Wace,Layamon and the authors of the Brut y Brenhinedd)
21 Isaac: Name – Genesis 21:3 -Source Dictionary of American Family Names -2013 Oxford University Press
22 Isaac: Name – Genesis 21:3 -Source Dictionary of American Family Names -2013 Oxford University Press
23 Dr. Carl Jung – statement
24 Shakespeare – Quote
25 Emily Elizabeth Dickinson, *I Felt a Funeral in my Brain*, (Public Domain, 1830-1886) Wikisource.org/wiki/Page: Emily Dickinson Poems p third series (1896).djvu/182
26 Alistair MacLeod – *No Great Mischief*
27 Merton, Thomas (1915-1968) – Conjectures of a Guilty Bystander, Merton Legacy Trust, The Thomas Center, Bellamine University, USAMerton
28 Pam Grout, *E-Squared*, (Hay House Inc. USA, 2013)
29 Debra Doerksen-Spiritual Mediumship -www.debradoerksen.com
30 Donna L. Gray, *Mindless Movement*
31 Mark Wolynn, *It Didn't Start with You*, (Viking, An Imprint of Penguin, Random House LLC, 2016)
32 Eileen Curteis, *The Dance of the Mystic Healer*, (Sisters of Saint Ann, Victoria, BC, 2001)
33 Eileen Curteis, *The Road to Compassion – Poem*
34 Francine Sharpiro, PhD., *Getting Past Your Past*, (Rodale Inc. New York, 2012)

35 William Blake – Quote
36 Aldous Huxley – Quote
37 Blue Jay Totem -www.spiritanimals.com
38 Paul Levy – Quote *Awaken Ina Dream, 2018*
39 Dimitri Nasrallah – *Niko* – (McCelland & Stewart)
40 Donna L. Gray, *Sodalite*, (Sooke, BC, 2017)
41 Pamela Ball, *10,000 Dreams Explained,* (London, UK, Arcturus Publishing, 2015)
42 Rev. Chris Michaels – Quote- Missouri Center for Spiritual Living, Kansas City
43 Sharlyn HiDalgo, *The Healing Power of Trees* (Llewllyn, MN, 2011)
44 Donna L. Gray, *Fire*, (Sooke, BC, 2017)
45 George Bernard Shaw – Quote
46 Anne Wilson Schaefer
47 Charlotte Bronte, *Life*, (Public Domain) (wiki source.org. wiki/Poems 1846, under Currer,Ells and Acton Bell/Life)

Lightning Source UK Ltd.
Milton Keynes UK
UKHW041450281218
334562UK00001B/56/P